DIVORCED VIRGIN

MY STORY OF HOW NOT TO GET SCREWED BY THE SYSTEM.

EVAN CUTLER
evancutlerauthor@gmail.com

Copyright © 2024 by Irfan Kutlu

All rights reserved.

No part of this book may be reproduced, distributed, or transmitted in any form or by any means, including photocopying, recording, or other electronic or mechanical methods, without the prior written permission of the publisher, except in the case of brief quotations embodied in critical reviews and certain other non-commercial uses permitted by copyright law.

For permission requests, please get in touch with the publisher at the address below:

9 Lives Publishing

Australia

Melbourne Victoria 3000

Email Address: authordivorcedvirgin@gmail.com

This is a work of nonfiction. While the experiences and events described in this book are true, names, characters, businesses, and locations may have been changed to protect the privacy of individuals. Any resemblance to actual persons, living or dead, is purely coincidental.

ISBN: 978-1-7637577-0-7 paperback
ISBN: 978-1-7637577-1-4 hard cover
ISBN: 978-1-7637577-2-1 EBOOK
ISBN: 978-1-7637577-3-8 AUDIO

Printed in AUSTRALIA

First Edition

DEDICATION

To my little boy, Kayra, you are my life's beacon of hope and joy—a precious gift born. Your laughter and first words fill my heart, reminding me that new beginnings are possible. I promise to always fight for a future where we can share our life adventures together.

There are a few truths I wish to share with you, insights drawn from my own journey—filled with both pain and joy.

As you grow, prioritize your own happiness and embrace your self-worth. Remember, you are strong and resilient. You will learn that you are more capable than you realise. Surround yourself with people who appreciate you and treat you with kindness. And don't be afraid to walk away should someone try to take that away from you.

Trust your instincts. Speak your truth. Relationships should give you peace, not turmoil. If something feels amiss, your heart whispers caution. Listen.

Love fiercely, but do not love your partner more than they love you. Learn to enjoy your own company, dive into your passions and pursue your dreams.

Create a life worth celebrating, filled with joy, fulfilment, and love.

With all my love,

Dad.

EPIGRAPH

"Ah, yes, Divorce .... from the Latin word meaning to rip out a man's genitals through his wallet."
Robin Williams

CONTENTS

INTRODUCTION 7

01. MY TRIAL WAS A FARCE! 13
02. DIVORCE IS BIG BUSINESS 21
03. IVOs 26
04. BACK IN COURT 34
05. FUCK SUICIDE! REVENGE IS BETTER 42
06. IT'S MY BUSINESS! 51
    Separating your finances 56

07. AMBUSHED 57
08. FIRST DAY IN COURT 65
09. LOVE STORY 74
    "The person you think they are." 74

10. DIVORCE and the SILVER BULLET 82
    UNDERHANDED DIVORCE TACTICS 82
    Fractured Alliances and Divorce Dynamics 86
    Lodging a caveat on matrimonial real property. ... 87
    Scare Tactics 87
    Blue Monsters 89

11. FIRST DAY IN COURT SELF REPRESENTED ... 94
    MEDIATION 104
    Dinner at Vue de Monde 113

12. PSYCHOLOGY OF DIVORCE 116
    The person they're now going to become in the family court. ... 117
    ANGER 118
    During the legal divorce or litigation stage.. 119
    Following the physical separation and the initiation
    of legal divorce proceedings. 119
    Financial and monetary worries 120
    the silent marriage 120
    Parental care concerns.. 122

Psychology of ego ego is a dirty word!.. 124
Love Story "The person they are." 126

13. LIQUIDATE THE BUSINESS! **135**
14. DEPRESSION **140**
15. THE APPEAL. **144**
　Errors of Law 146
　Errors of Fact 146
　Procedural Fairness 146
　Significant Legal Issues 147
　Meritorious Grounds. 147
　Judicial Discretion 147
　Appropriate Relief.. 147
　APPLICATION TO THE FULL COURT 149
　Filing a Notice of Appeal.. 149
　Preparation of Appeal Book 150
　FULL COURT APPEAL GRANTED 154

16. SCATTER GUN AT BEST! **157**
17. LOVE STORY **159**
　"The person they become in (~~Family Court~~)"
　　　　the UNDERWORLD. 159

18. COVID. **165**
　Ok! It's Mid-Life Crisis Time 166
　Dunes of The Cape 173

19. FINAL CHAPTER **176**

AFTERWORD **178**

INTRODUCTION

AUTHOR

Divorced Virgin is just not another divorce book. It's a brutally honest, sometimes absurdly funny, and deeply personal account of my journey through a broken system that seems designed to break men. This book is written for men who, like me, found themselves lost in the chaos of divorce with no guide, no support, and certainly no sympathy from a system stacked against them. While countless books are written by women, for women — empowering them through divorce and life afterward — men are left to fend for themselves. When I needed guidance, I found none, so I decided to write the book I wish had existed.

My experience with divorce was a nightmare that spanned over 50 court appearances, 44 of which I represented myself. Walking into that courtroom time and time again felt like stepping into a circus complete with absurd performances and manipulative theatrics designed to destroy my credibility and drain my spirit. I quickly learned that family court was not about fairness or truth, but survival. The person I thought I had married turned into someone unrecognisable in the courtroom —battling me with lies and false accusations to win at all costs. Family court became the arena where this third version of my ex-wife showed up, and it was more vicious than I could have imagined.

But amidst the chaos and the legal absurdities, I found something unexpected: humour. Sometimes, the only way to deal with the madness is to laugh at it. The outrageous claims, the non-sensical procedures, and the emotionally charged courtroom antics became so absurd that humour became my greatest defence. This book isn't just venting frustrations; it explores how you can find your strength and even your sense of humour in the darkest moments.

I wrote Divorced Virgin to give voice to the male divorce experience, a perspective often ignored. Men aren't supposed to talk about their pain, their failures, or their frustrations with the legal system. We're expected to endure it in silence. But silence keeps us isolated, allowing the system to continue unchecked. I refuse to be silent. I refuse to be a victim of the system. And I refuse to let other men go through what I went through without at least the benefit of my hindsight and hard-earned lessons. This story is about reclaiming your dignity, finances, and sanity in a world that seems determined to strip you of all three. Yes, you'll read about the brutal realities of divorce–how men are often sidelined, how the system seems rigged–but you'll also read about how to navigate these waters without losing yourself. I hope this book will offer practical advice and serve as a source of empowerment, humour, and resilience.

This book is for you if you're facing divorce or are already in the trenches. It's for the men who feel unseen and unheard, the fathers fighting for their children, and anyone who needs a laugh at the absurdity of it all. Divorce might take a lot from you, but it doesn't have to take everything. Protect your sense of self, your sense of humour, and above all, your Divorce Virginity.

PROLOGUE
DIVORCED VIRGIN

My story of how not to get screwed by the system.

When my ex-wife filed for divorce, I experienced an epiphany: You don't marry just one person. You really marry three: the person you think they are, the person they actually are, and the person they will become in Family Court.

Divorced Virgin is about you and the third person you didn't know you married.

Family court is where you get screwed by the third one once the other two stops screwing you in bed. Two famous quotes to best understand the third version of your spouse are:

"Hell, Hath No Fury Like a Women Scorned" and
"Nothing in the world is more dangerous than sincere ignorance and conscientious stupidity."

I cannot decide which of the phrases above can do the most harm.

I have long wondered what the first meant. I have heard it before, but I never gave it too much thought. To me, it sounded Shakespearean. Man, was I wrong!

The quote was taken from the play. "Love for Love" by an English playwright, William Congreve, in 1695. (At least I got the William part right.) Let's break it down to understand it:

HELL is a place or state of torment and punishment in an afterlife.

HATH is the present tense of have or has.

FURY means great anger.

SCORNED is to treat or regard with contempt or disdain.

In other words, HELL HATH NO FURY really means that even Hell does not have anger sufficiently great to compare to a really pissed-off female.

Sounds really brutal, comparing the behaviour of women being worse than hell.

As for the second quote, it's from one of the most respected men to ever live on this planet: Martin Luther King, Jr. When King said this, he was explaining the rationalisation of enslavement.

Blacks were thought to be inferior and thus deserving of their fate.

Everyone "knew" it and challenging the idea would get you in trouble. In fact, at one time, people were persecuted because they said the Earth was round when everyone "knew" it was flat. Saying that the Earth was not the centre of the Universe put your life at risk. I first read that quote printed on a T-shirt.

So, how are both these quotes relevant to your divorce proceedings?

Let's start with DIVORCE LAWYERS!

Jean Kerr couldn't have said it any better: -

"A lawyer is never entirely comfortable with a friendly divorce, any more than a good mortician wants to finish his job and then have the patient sit up on the table."

In my initial meeting with my Divorce Lawyer, I was quoted a line from Robin Williams.

"Ah, yes, Divorce …. from the Latin word meaning to rip out a man's genitals through his wallet."

You may need to hire a bankruptcy lawyer after your Divorce Lawyer finishes with you.

You wouldn't be the first and certainly not the last to think that divorce could never have happened to you. After all, when you were married, you had your own hidden prejudices about divorced people. You thought you were better than they were and would never be one of "them." You probably even felt that divorced people just hadn't tried enough to work on their relationship. It certainly wasn't a part of your life plan.

Welcome to the Family. It's a group of men who have reached their breaking point, driven to desperation by a system that bankrupted them and destroyed their families, a history of men dousing themselves in gasoline and lighting themselves a blaze at the doorstep of the courthouse though hardly anyone seemed to have noticed.

Divorced Virgin is not that story. It breaks the family curse, so you don't get screwed!

The promises of wedding vows with the best intentions get tested when life — past and present — shows up.

Much is invested in wedding preparations, while divorce statistics starkly contrast with wedding day bliss. And as you know, many marriages do not last today.

When a marriage is in crisis, love is stretched, faith is tested, and, sadly, respect may be lost.

As common as divorce is today, few really want divorce to be a part of their story or to be known as someone who seemingly "failed" in this aspect of life. When a relationship fails, it is nearly always a hard fight. Do not internalise failure into a permanent fixture of your identity. Fight for this truth: Your worthiness to receive love and belonging is not up for negotiation. Shame should never be elicited by divorce, which is far from the beginning of an end. My story is different from yours, and yours is different from others. There is a multitude of reasons why a marriage ends; your story is unique.

At the time of writing **Divorced Virgin,** this was far from my lowest point of self-worth. When women and men divorce, when they dispute custody of children, and when they battle over property, things get bitter and contested. **And Men get screwed over in divorce court**.

The Family Courts are beset by problems flooded with false accusations of abuse against men, accusations to win custody battles and to benefit her share of the matrimonial asset pool. This situation is exacerbated, as was the case for me when the Chief Justice can ring up a mate and offer a judgeship to someone with minimal Family Law experience. Most Australians would think that for a Judge to get the top job, they must undergo a rigorous review process. That is not the case! The entire system is a circus, and it's up to you to learn how to perform in the ring. Your virginity as a divorcee cannot be protected with "ignorance and conscientious stupidity."

My name is Evan Cutler, and at the end of this book, I successfully become a DIVORCED VIRGIN.

CHAPTER 1
MY TRIAL WAS A FARCE!

It was a Wednesday morning, the 06th of November. Derby Day, in fact.

An incredible event that combines sport, fashion and food all in one place.

Whilst the rest of Melbourne was engulfed in horse racing and carnival spirit, men enmeshed in Family Court proceedings are prepping to be either shorn or stripped entirely of their money, homes and families.

The stakes are high, with hundreds of thousands of dollars and sometimes millions on the line. These stakes unsurprisingly drive people to lie. Lies are at the messy heart of divorce. The lies can be so significant that lawyers and judges often have to officiate death matches of he-said-she-said.

If you have ever passed through metal detectors at airports, you're already familiar with the process of emptying your pockets, isolating your notebooks and iPads from your bag or briefcase, and putting your bag and briefcase in a large plastic tub on a conveyor belt ready to be scanned for any explosives, machetes, pistols, and machine guns that we may have inadvertently forgotten to leave in the trunk or boot of our car or basement at home.

It is certainly not our intention to subvert the prominent paradigm.

As I waited this fateful day, two barristers behind me were discussing the details of some sworn testimony a scorned wife was scheduled to give later that day about her relationship with her abusive husband.

We were all herded through the detectors without any order of succession. The right of succession does not start until we reach the other side of the metal detectors. As I wrote earlier, you must be careful not to place anything hazardous in the plastic tub, as any shift in the paradigm (perish the thought!) would be nothing short of a cataclysm comparable to the First World War.

Once given the all-clear, I walked left to the Daily Court List, looked up my name and duly proceeded to level 4, courtroom 4X, as indicated on the list-.

Justice W. Smallcock was presiding.

Julia, my wife, walked in with her usual entourage. McKenzie friend Mr M Wank, her sister Ebrill, her ugly friend Fat Bertrude, Fat Bertrude's house cleaner, sister-in-law, and Fat Bertrude's mother. My wife Julia and her friend Mr M Wank proceeded to sit behind the bench in front of the court clerks whilst the rest of her entourage found their places in the gallery.

This is now where the right of succession takes form.

In a typical courtroom, the judge sits behind a raised desk known as the bench. Adjacent to the bench are the witness stand on one side and the desks where the court clerks sit on the other. The courtroom is divided into two parts by an imaginary barrier known as the bar. There is an open space between the bench and the counsel tables. If documents must be given or taken from the Judge, barristers are typically expected to approach the court clerk.

I walked in on my own, took my usual seat to the right of the same bench and leaned back on my chair until three slow knocks from the judge's chamber sounded out.

(Remember the right of succession I mentioned?)

"Silence in Court. All stand" We all stood.

"This Honourable Court is now in session", announced the Clerk.

Each time I heard the three knocks, I remembered an old wives' tale concerning the three knocks of death. If you hear three knocks on the door and nobody's there when you answer, someone close to you is supposedly going to die. And if several deaths occur in the same family, you tie a black ribbon to everything left alive that enters the house, even dogs and chickens.

The judge entered and walked to his chair. He then bowed, everybody else bowed, and the judge sat.

"Please be seated," announced the Clerk, and everyone in court sat.

My wife Julia then stood and announced that she was the defendant representing herself, and then I stood and announced that I was the applicant without representation.

As this was our 43rd session, we were now well-accustomed to the court procedures.

Yes, you read right! The 43rd fucking session!

"Ms Cutler, I'm ready to hear your arguments regarding your application," says Justice W. Smallcock.

Julia stood and immediately turned on the floodgates for the waterworks.

"Your Honour," she began before pausing and catching her breath. What a performance.

She gasped and continued, "Your Honour, I'm sorry, but I'm so nervous. " Wiping away her crocodile tears, she'd perfected this strategy throughout the past five years leading up to these proceedings.

"Since the separation, the applicant has left me destitute. He continues to ignore the orders of this court, and now I'm forced to fend for myself and my three children. He took over the business directorship without my consent, leaving me penniless. Furthermore, I've just realised he's now commenced additional proceedings in Spain concerning our holiday house on the coast, and I don't have the means to defend my right of title. He has no consideration for his children and no respect for this court."

She now bursts into a hysterical fit and supposedly uncontrollable crying. Her McKenzie friend Mr M Wank stood and consoled her, then asked Judge W. Smallcock for a moment for Julia to recompose herself.

Justice W Smallcock then looked at me and waited for me to respond.

"Mr Cutler, what do you say about your application in the case that will convince me to stay my previous orders?" Justice W. Smallcock asked.

I remained silent, eyes closed and calmly began my breathing exercises, a relaxing technique taught to me after recently experiencing a minor stroke.

"Mr Cutler?" Justice W Smallcock repeated.

Slowly breathing in, then exhaling. I opened my eyes, turned my head towards Julia and her McKenzie friend Mr M Wank and began to clap slowly. If you don't know the meaning of this, slow clapping is widely used as a popular dramatic device, usually accompanied by ironic dialogue such as "well done" or "Bravo" to indicate disbelief or show scorn.

"That performance your Honour is truly worthy of an Oscar."

Judge W. Smallcock cut me short with, "Mr Cutler, your application is for a stay of my Orders of the Final Trial. What are your arguments?"

"Your Honour," I replied, always remaining composed,

"your trial has been nothing but a farce." I continued.

At this stage, it wasn't difficult to see that Justice W Smallcock was becoming annoyed.

"I take offence to your comment, Mr Cutler," he said fumed.

"By calling it a farce, you're displaying a lack of respect for me and this court !"

Respect?

Let me talk about respect for a moment, **Dear Reader**, with a sidebar on my mother; may she rest in peace. In her heyday, she was a maiden with an iron fist. She was strict because of her cultural traditions. She was a taskmaster, mission maker and decider of everyone's general direction in life. Her expectations of me were exceedingly high, though she provided little nurturance. Her feedback for me was often negative. More than once, she threw her slipper from across the room smack on target to the back of my head or gave firm and unyielding swings of the pastry roller onto my arse as I attempted to outrun her for dear life.

I grew more robust as the years passed, and she became slower. The slippers and pastry roller became a distant memory. But she refused to fit the stereotype of the doddering, depressed pensioner and likened herself to a sophist. Her devotion to the truth was beyond question. Her take on respect was simple.

If you want respect, then learn to give it!

"Offence is not intended, your honour," I replied, when in fact, **Dear Reader**, you and I both know it absolutely was.

"I've taken the liberty of printing the definition of farce this morning," holding the printed page with one hand, the other hand in my trouser pocket, imitating what can probably be best described as the Perry Mason look and proceeded to read out what, of course, suited me…

The Collins definition goes as follows:

> *"A farce is a broad satire or comedy, though now it's used to describe something that is supposed to be serious but has turned ridiculous."*

I read a slightly different version :

> *"If a defendant is not treated fairly, his lawyer might say that the trial is a farce."*

I claimed this to be an Oxford dictionary definition, fully conversant that it was not.

"Furthermore!" I continued, raising my tone for a more dramatic effect.

"Her affidavits are just as implausible as the 1001 Tales of The Arabian Nights!"

"Sit down, Mr Cutler!" exclaimed Justice W. Smallcock, his face flushed crimson.

Smallcock then turned his attention back to Julia.

"Ms Cutler, are you now in a better mindset? Have you composed yourself, and can you continue, please?"

"Yes, thank you, your Honour," she replied— a remarkable portrait of dignified strength.

"It recently came to my attention that the respondent has started a new company, guising it under his de facto girlfriend's name." His girlfriend has just arrived from Spain, where she was previously an English teacher. She cannot possibly know how to run a business of this nature."

"**Objection, Your Honour**!" I exclaimed.

"She is not my girlfriend, and no one has arrived from Spain! Furthermore, these accusations are irrelevant to this court, and the applicant's comments are only hearsay"!

Now hearsay, my **Dear Reader**, is an essential court term that simply means gossip.

"Sit down, Mr Cutler! You'll have your chance."

"I won't warn you again!" snapped Smallcock.

"He clearly intends to transfer the business assets to this new company of his girlfriend to avoid paying the business debts to the banks!" continued my wife innocently.

"Your Honour! She's referring to phoenixing!" I interrupted once again.

"It's where she claims I transfer over assets from one company to another to avoid paying financiers and creditors. But this is a moot point because, regardless of the registered owner of the assets, the banks have lien on the vehicles until the debt owed is discharged!"

And I sat back down.

At this point, I was aghast at the silence.

No one was talking. Justice Smallcock didn't even ask me to shut up.

So, I stood back up again, projecting plenty of confidence and continued.

"Furthermore, your Honour, she cannot be appointed director as this was already covered in prior trials! Judge Reinhold concluded that the applicant did not possess the necessary accreditation."

"Your Honour, as I said previously, and I'll say again, your courtroom is a farce!"

"We should not even be here listening to her crap again!"

Apparently, Judge Smallcock was not in agreement with this assessment.

"One more outburst, Mr Cutler, and I'll have you handcuffed and thrown out of my courtroom!" he threatened.

"It's been five years to the day today, and we're back to square one!" I protested with a raised voice.

"You're nothing but a circus ringmaster!"

Justice W. Smallcock then exploded.

"Mr Cutler! I'll have you for contempt of court and incarcerate you for a period of my choosing!" vociferously opposing my rebellious demeanour.

"You have no idea how to do your job!" I bellowed.

Defensively, with his stiff-necked pride, he threatened to leave the courtroom.

Now reader. I swallowed all that anger when it was a fire seed and forgot to drink something cool; it erupted within me until it emerged as scorching as the fieriest breath ever unleashed by a dragon on the person I knew to be a cantankerous, easily annoyed, pugnacious fuck. Justice W Smallcock.

I breathed fire and let fly.

"I shit turds that are bigger than you!"

I'll never forget his eyes, how that fire burnt him to ash.

In accordance with his dignity, both fists slamming the bench, enraged, he stood and deserted his place.

The sudden quiet grew, and I felt every beat pound in my chest.

The look on the clerk's face was one of awkwardness.

"So, what do we do now?" I asked the clerk. "How long is he going to sook out the back for?"

No answer was forthcoming.

"Well, we may as well all go home then. I have better things to do," I continued.

Instinctively, I turned back to the gallery. Only then did I realise how many other people were in there. The gallery was packed. Barristers, lawyers, families of litigants, ex Wives, and the men who were about to be screwed were all waiting for their case to be next heard.

All eyes were on me, their mouths gaping. My brain stuttered momentarily, but the anger lingered regardless, still flaming hot. Beverly Ripp, a senior barrister who once represented Julia, was sitting opposite where I was left standing. She was white as chalk. Her eyes and mouth were frozen wide open in an expression of stunned surprise, and although she was staring straight at me, she appeared not to notice me.

Leaning over slightly, I whispered.

"Excuse me love. Would you like me to get you a bag of popcorn?"

CHAPTER 2
DIVORCE IS BIG BUSINESS

Zsa Zsa Gabor was once quoted as saying.

"Diamonds are a girl's best friend, and dogs are a man's best friend. Now you know which sex has more sense."

Divorce is becoming increasingly commonplace, ravaging our society. The figures are staggering. One in three Australian marriages, 42% of English marriages and 55% of American marriages end in divorce. When Julia first filed for divorce, I was determined to find the best Goddamn lawyer I could. Five years ago, like you, I knew little about the system beyond what I'd heard from people around me. —A friend once told me his wife woke beside him, turned to him and spoke…

"Zack, I just don't feel the spark between us anymore. I want a divorce."

"What was your reply?" I asked.

"I told her to go and sit on a power pole!" he replied.

Another friend, Harry, once told me his wife also wanted a divorce. He was expected to leave the house and find alternative accommodation. He refused. So, one evening after a night out with the boys, he returned home somewhat intoxicated and lumbered straight onto the couch, only to be woken by thuds banging on his front door.

(No, they weren't the three knocks.)

When he opened his eyes, two police officers were standing right beside him, telling him he had 5 minutes to pack his shit together and get out. In the time he was asleep, presumably sobering, his wife called the Police and told them her husband came home dead drunk, abused her verbally, and now she feared for her safety.

"The Police just can't do that!" I said sceptically, thinking Harry must not be telling me the whole story.

You're probably thinking what I thought at the time. Surely, there must be more to it. There are rules, and there are laws. They can't do that, can they?

Well, <u>Dear Reader</u>, I can tell you that they most certainly can, and they most certainly did it to me. Julia and I were constantly fighting, but divorce was the furthest thing from my mind. I don't remember the specifics of our arguments, but I will never forget the months of silent torture I would always endure in the aftermath. Irrespective of the irrelevance of the nature of our bickering, she could completely be oblivious to our coexistence. Until, of course, we reached the point where she decided to cross that line and crush me under the wheels of "justice."

I first heard of Pitt, Bull & Associates on my car radio.

We all know that "Family" is a popular symbol in commercial advertising.

The ad was convincing.

"We understand the most important thing in the world is family. Here at Pitt, Bull and Associates, we always put you and your family first. You will never go wrong nor have any regrets," the ad said.

It was ironic that divorce lawyers tried to sell themselves on family values. Wasn't divorce antithetical to our perception of both family and values?

I emailed my business lawyer and asked if he knew much about this firm.

"They're character assassins!" was his reply.

Sounded good to me. The first consultation was free, so I made the call and booked my appointment.

As I sat in the outer office waiting, I could see into the offices of some of the lawyers in this firm. Two distinctively more prominent offices were partially in sight. Sketched onto the windows in silver letters was the word Partner on each of the two larger offices. One had a male, and the other office had a female. The sign behind the receptionist announced in bold silver block lettering:

Pitt, Bull and Associates

I figured I would get Pitt, and I did. I deduced that Bull was the female assassin the firm referred to as the other partner.

However, reputation aside, my first session with Joe Pitt was uninformative, and my initial thoughts of him were unimpressive. He was definitely not the Perry Mason I had envisaged—more like Columbo. He was of short stature, unkempt, and untidy.

Only during my second consultation did it become intriguing.

He opened by asking, "Does she have access to your bank accounts"?

"Yes," I replied.

"You need to remove her," he brusquely continued

"Well, how would she live?" I asked, foolishly concerned.

"Sometimes people come in with the most unbelievable sob stories because they didn't listen. I don't put myself through all that hard work just to mop up disasters of their own making," he said.

"You're worried how she's going to live? Fuck her! You'll be kissing my ass when this is all over."

He grinned. "We're going to decimate her and her lawyers !" he proclaimed confidently.

I shifted position in my chair and began to tap my knees rhythmically—a tell of my anxiety.

A flashback of Donald Trump hosting The Apprentice leapt to mind. He would point at one of the two last remaining contestants after tearing themselves apart in a heart-breaking effort to win his approval and say, "You're Hired!" I wasn't about to be that dramatic. Instead, I simply said.

"I like you."

Now, keep in mind that divorce is big business. An old saying goes, "One person's loss is another person's gain." Divorce lawyers have known this for many years and have done very well indeed. Australia's longest, messiest, and most expensive divorce was a 14-year saga that rang up

$40 million in legal fees. The appeal judges noted in their decision that the couple had been "litigating about their marriage longer than they had been married." The women burned through "approximately 16 different firms of solicitors, eight different senior counsels and 14 different junior counsels." ...Each, in turn, either ceased to act or alternatively, had their services terminated," Justice Paul Cronin noted.

The national economy incurs over $14 billion annually in government assistance payments and court expenses due to divorce and family breakdowns. Divorce lawyers take in $185 million in revenue each year. That's why good bankruptcy lawyers are typically sought once your divorce lawyer is finished with you.

The bottom line is that this wouldn't come cheap. Joe Pitt from Pitt Bull and Associates asked for a $20000.00 deposit to be placed in trust. He informed me that he wouldn't do any work until there was money set aside for it.

"You may not need to spend all of that, but I'm not a charity," he blurted out.

"We need the money on the table in case things get complicated."

"What is this going to cost in total?" I asked warily. I assumed that the twenty thousand must be a safety net, an overly large figure designed to cover even unusually large bills and that my actual total would be much less.

"Well, I don't know!" If it's a straightforward divorce, then $3000.00." He paused, and I waited for the other shoe to drop. "If it gets messy, maybe thirty, fifty thousand..." he continued. Yep. There it was.

As I walked back to my car from the offices of Pitt Bull and Associates, a bit shell-shocked, I felt a sense of forlornness. A realisation that my family's life journey was now separated from my own; the only heart beating in my world now is that of my own. The very definition of provider is well-ingrained in our society, and my mother undoubtedly built it into the foundations of my psyche. How was I supposed to cut off Julia's access to the bank accounts? Now that I think about it, how dare Pitt say, "Fuck her!"

Disorientated, I decided to text Julia.

I want to point out here that Apple, with the explosion of the iPhone, changed the world. Changing the world meant changing how we approached many things, but ultimately, it proved easily achievable. The iPhone 4 only had a 3.5-inch display, and I had just started to need reading glasses. Distraction weakens our memories, and consequently, we are more prone to forgetting things. I, for one, always forgot where my reading glasses were.

Auto-correct and dictate were technologies just in their infancy at that time. I am a complete technophobe, but I undertook the task of using the dictate function. So, I dictated. This proved to be a mistake.

I said;

> "Julia. Can we try to work things out without Lawyers"?
> "He's the male partner assassin only interested in decimating you."
> "My Lawyer said it could cost up to $50K".

Auto correct sent it as:

> "Julia, can we try to work things out without Lawyers?
> "The male assassin is only interested in decimating you."
> "Larry said it could cost up to $50K".

She responded almost instantaneously with

> "That sounds Like a threat to me!
> I'm reporting you to the Police!
> You've just breached your Intervention Order and will be hearing from my Lawyers!"

Thanks for nothing, Apple.

CHAPTER 3
IVOs

"Once Upon a time," your marriage was probably the highlight of your life- and now, if you're reading my book, you or somebody you know is likely to be experiencing marital problems. The journey together didn't exactly end up "happily ever after." Contrary to common belief, men going through a divorce are just as, if not more, hurt than women. Divorce is mentally exhausting and emotionally exasperating. By reading my story, I hope you will benefit from my experiences and remain a Divorced Virgin. In other words, you can avoid getting screwed by the system!

You're not alone. You won't be the first, and you surely won't be the last person to separate. Realise that divorce happens to the best of us. I am still living with one foot in the past and am likely to relive all the mistakes that occurred during my marriage for the rest of my life. One such mistake involved the police issuing me an IVO order.

An IVO is an abbreviation of an Intervention Order (in America, they call this a "Restraining Order"). Its purpose is to protect a person from a family member who is using violence. Unquestionably, I don't condone violence, especially within the home. Nevertheless, I've yet to meet a man who has not been served an IVO, either just before or amid a divorce. Inexcusably, wives and female partners who are not subjected to family violence unforgivably attempt to abuse the process for their benefit, either to apply for an adjustment to their entitlement during the trial or sometimes to spite the father by impeding access to his children. Imperatively, you must avoid this process at all costs. I didn't, and I paid dearly for my error.

To my female readers, don't give up on me just yet! I'm not a man who believes that men are superior to women. I simply oppose the legal paradigm of the Family Law system, which takes the side of women over men by default. Though historically, issues of domestic abuse and child neglect have somewhat been characterised as male issues, if you continue to read on, you will see that all men cannot be put into the same basket.

Looking back with the benefit of hindsight, what was to come should have been obvious. Julia drove me to the airport the morning I left for Spain to attend to legal matters concerning our coastal home. Nothing out of the ordinary, except this time, she didn't park her car at the terminal and remain with me until just before I boarded my flight. She only got out of her vehicle long enough to stuff a jar of coffee into my luggage, which she had forgotten to pack, intended for her brother, who was then residing in Spain. I remember the drive to the airport as being awkward, as neither of us had much to say to the other. With the jar of coffee now securely arranged in my luggage, she said bye, waved at me, got back into her car and sped off. Not exactly an emotional display, though not overly hostile either. But when I returned, after a stay in Spain that was not without incidents, the shit hit the fan.

During my absence, she had changed the locks of our home and refused to let me in. I also had no money; she had stopped all my company credit and debit cards. I didn't even have internet banking access; she had changed the passwords and removed me from the accounts altogether. You should by now be curious about how she could accomplish all that, considering I was the business director, right?

Surprise, surprise: she removed me as director and changed the shareholding of the business to her name. As of that moment, I was officially penniless and homeless. Later, I discovered that she'd also changed the title of our home from joint names to that of her own, just two weeks before my mother passed away after a nine-month battle with pancreatic cancer.

Though I'd been sympathetic to the homeless until this all transpired, I never understood how people resorted to sleeping on park benches and under bridges. Surely, being homeless in the most liveable city in the world can only be the result of their own doing.

Picture this: It was now 11:15 p.m., in the middle of winter. I was locked out of my home, penniless, and without access to any of my accounts. Standing next to my suitcase full of dirty laundry on the porch, I took the phone out of my coat pocket and called the police.

"Moonee Ponds Police Senior Sargent Dyke speaking," answered someone.

"Hello?" I began.

"Police?" Stupidly, I thought, who else could it be, considering I placed the call?

"You've called Moonee Ponds Police. What is the nature of your call ?" she continued.

"I've come home, and my wife has changed the locks."

"She won't let me in the house."

"Has there been any violence?" asked Senior Sargent Dyke

"No, there hasn't", I replied patiently.

"Can I break down the door and go in?"

"Definitely not; you can't do that."

"What's the address? I'll send a unit down. You must remain calm and not do anything; just wait for us to arrive," was her reply.

After providing Senior Sargent Dyke with the address, I hung up and waited patiently. An hour passed by, and they still didn't show. So, I called again.

She told me again how busy they were, that I was to remain as I was and continue to be patient, and hung up on me.

Now annoyed with me still standing on the front porch, Julia yelled through the lead-glass window for me to go or she'd call the police. She obviously didn't know that that was precisely what I was trying to do.

"I'm not leaving!" I insisted.

"That's it! I'm calling the Police!" she declared.

I smirked, thinking that being the first to call would somehow give me greater credibility when they eventually arrived. But then, a police car pulled in within minutes of her call! Now think what you may think, Reader. I still don't think of it as a coincidence that I'd been waiting for an hour, and Julia got a response within minutes.

"Sir! Please step away from the door. I'm Senior Sergeant Dyke, and this is Constable Sapphic. What seems to be the problem?" she demanded.

"She's changed the locks and won't let me into my home", I replied.

Constable Sapphic then told me that she and Senior Constable Dyke would go inside to speak to my wife and that I was to remain outside. After 15 minutes they both returned and asked me to whom the suitcase belonged. I told them that it was mine and I had just returned from Spain to – as I'd already said several times- find the locks had been changed.

"Well, sir," Dyke said sternly.

"You need to return from where you've just come from," pointing to the front gate.

"What?" I was so surprised I thought I had misheard her.

"You need to vacate the property immediately, " Sapphic affirmed.

"What are you talking about? I live here, and this is my house!" I protested.

"No, you don't live here, and this is no longer your house; now, please get off the property. She no longer wants you here!" said the officer.

"Where am I supposed to go? I don't even have any money; she blocked my access to the business accounts and my cards," I pleaded.

"That's not our concern. It would be best if you left now, or I'll issue you an IVO and arrest you," was her response.

I had no idea what an IVO was, but I did remember the time that Harry told me the police gave him five minutes to get his shit together and leave his home. I should have been more sympathetic towards him instead of being so cynical. Fuck! The same thing was happening to me, but I was determined not to leave until I put up a decent fight.

"I'm not going anywhere! Try and drag me out!" I dared them. Surely, they wouldn't throw me off my own property. I still did not believe that Julia could do this.

Within seconds of my dare, Dyke immediately took out her baton and radioed in for backup whilst Sapphic started to write up the IVO!

My face dropped faster than a corpse in cement boots. The backup came screeching up the road, as subtle as a freshly popped zit and just as welcome. The red and blue lights of two police cars flashed brightly in the gathering gloom and drew the attention of all the neighbours. This wasn't some inner-city dive. We lived in leafy suburbia, and the cops only came there to check out errant house alarms and the odd break-in. I could see my ragdoll cat, Aslan, stretched out with his underbelly pressed up against the window facing the porch, scratching frantically from inside the dining room. Constable Mutt, accompanied by Constable Jeff, joined Senior Constable Dyke and Constable Sapphic on the front lawn whilst I just stood beside my suitcase full of dirty laundry.

Dyke and Mutt approached me and asked if I knew what an IVO is. I replied that I did not, so they explained to me what an Interim Family Violence Intervention Order is and how it now prohibited me from contacting Julia and my children.

"What Violence?!" I yelled. "I'm the one who called you! You can't throw me out of my own home!"

One of the most recognisable strategies used by police is one you're probably familiar with: the good cop / bad cop technique. Whilst Dyke and Mutt pulled out the Pepper Sprays, Jeff and Sapphic took the opposing sympathetic approach.

"Listen, mate, you can't be here," said Constable Jeff in what he thought passed for a reasonable tone. "You can't contact her either; if you attempt to make any form of contact, you will be arrested and prosecuted. You need to get out of here, and you need to get a lawyer. It will be costly, but you don't have any other choice."

"But I wasn't violent! I've just been standing here for the past two hours." I tried to tell him.

He shook his head sympathetically. "Look, you need to tell it to the judge. This is an Interim Violence Order. You'll have your chance in three days when you appear at the Magistrates Court in Broadmeadows."

If there had ever been any hope of Julia and me trying to work out our issues, even if only a tiny flicker, it died on this night. Some people fear clowns, some heights, or falling. Not me. I am not scared of spiders, snakes, or even the police. What I fear most is loneliness. Escorted into a cab with my suitcase full of dirty laundry, exhausted and smelling of body odour, the driver asked, "Where to?"

I had no clue.

My body was tense, and my brain was in a violent whirl of stupidity, trying to organise the unfolding chaos into anything that made sense. Within the scramble of my confusion, a 1986 earworm, "Driving Away from Home" by Immaterial, came to mind.

"Driving away from home.

Drivin'...

Driving away from home."

I never saw my home again after that night, even when Julia's lawyers eventually forced her to sell my castle. Driving away from home on that miserable night, I knew things were bad. Still, I could never have predicted how Julia would completely bleed the system by taking absolute advantage of the IVO and shed misery on my life.

The taxi driver eventually took me to my office, where my car was parked. I had left it in the warehouse before my trip to Spain. Technically, I wasn't supposed to enter the building as I was no longer the owner, and Julia now had an Intervention order preventing me from doing so. But the car was still mine, and I saw no other way to get it. Tossing my suitcase full of dirty laundry into the tiny boot of my 2-seat SL 500, I drove away and eventually into a supermarket carpark, which became my home for the following two nights. Without access to my cards or company accounts, I had no other alternative.

If stress is a coffee cup, and the cup spills, then it makes sense to put a lid on that cup. My lid was my personal assistant Samantha. I had first interviewed Samantha right after she graduated from university after completing her marketing degree. Samantha has a remarkably similar personality to Donna from the American legal drama Suits, played by Roberta Paulen. Like Donna, Samantha proved that awesomeness is a workplace skill. She always knew precisely where to find any documents before I knew I needed them and placed them neatly piled on my desk before I arrived for work each morning. I trusted Samantha completely, so much so that she was even a signatory to the company chequebook. So, if there was anyone who could help me out at that moment, I was sure it was Samantha.

Luxuriating in my new abode in the supermarket carpark, I waited patiently until 9:05 a.m. I knew Samantha would be in at precisely 9:00 a.m. (you could set your watch by her) and calculated five minutes to prepare her ritual morning coffee after she bid good morning to all the other staff on her way to her office. At 9:05 on the dot, I called her.

"Good morning, Samantha," I started like every other morning routine call. But this time, I had no intention of discussing the day's business tasks.

"Hey, I see you're back. Welcome back," she replied, noticing that my number didn't show an overseas prefix on her phone's display.

"Samantha…." I hesitated, not sure what to say. Then my brain kicked into gear.

"I need you to find the company register and email me a copy of the corporate key."

A corporate key, <u>Dear Reader</u>, is an 8-digit number uniquely linked to the company. It's like a bank account's PIN.

"The corporate key is not in the register; it's filed in the third cabinet, the second drawer with your contracts," Samantha instantly replied.

Wondering how exactly she knew, I revealed to my trusty assistant how Julia had changed the locks of my home, made herself director of the business, stopped my debit and credit cards, and cut me off from Internet banking.

"Well, as far as I'm concerned, and I'm certain everyone else thinks the same, you're the rightful owner, and you continue to be my boss. I'll start to make enquiries about how we can get you back. Leave it to me. In the meantime, I'll arrange to change the locks of the building to ensure Julia no longer has access," she said. Bless her. At that time, Samantha was my favourite person in the world.

I asked Samantha to write me a cash cheque right away for $6,000. I didn't know how long it would take to reinstate me as director, and I couldn't spend another night in my car parked in a supermarket carpark. To my immense relief, she agreed right away.

That same afternoon, she withdrew the $6,000 and prepared two Statutory Declarations stating that Julia's change of directorship and shareholding was not authorised. One was signed by her, and the other by Gabby, another employee. She also arranged an urgent meeting with ASIC (Australian Securities and Investment Commission).

A Statutory Declaration, Dear Reader, is a written statement declared true in the presence of an authorised witness. By signing it, you agree that the information in it is accurate. If the information turns out to be false, you can be charged with a criminal offence. If proceedings are underway with the Family Court, an affidavit is the better option.

Armed with the documents sent by Samantha, I headed to the meeting. I had the money now to get a hotel room, but there was no time to get cleaned up. Shortly filled with the vague stress of anticipation, the folder with the company constitution clenched tightly under my armpit, the two original copies of the Statutory Declaration signed by Samantha and Gabby in my hand and wafting the heavy stench of my body odour in all directions, I walked into the offices of ASIC.

The office was painted grey, with only one floor-to-ceiling window facing the courtyard opposite the trendy cafes of Collins Street. Behind the grey counter sat a desktop computer and a neat display of ASIC Forms behind the desk. Sweat started to trickle down from my forehead, but it wasn't because the central heating was blasting. A few pens were lying about, each attached by a delicate chain to the top of the counter. Always' s a sign of trust when they lock up a fifty-cent pen.

A pretty Asian girl approached the counter and asked how she could help me.

Where to begin.

I was as nervous as a pregnant nun. If I couldn't get my business back…

I was screwed.

CHAPTER 4
BACK IN COURT

Here Comes Judgment Day

The Clerk knocked on the door three times, indicating Justice W. Smallcock was about to return to the courtroom. I pictured Beverly Ripp with her eyes and mouth frozen wide open, looking around the gallery and checking if anyone had a black ribbon tied to them.

"Silence in court. All stand" There was the usual rustle of aggravated people shuffling to their feet for the millionth time.

"This Honourable Court is now in session," announced the Clerk, and Justice W. Smallcock walked to his chair and sat down. No bowing this time.

Judge Smallcock's demeanour was entirely automatic. His usual fake smile acquired a hint of ugly reality as he prepared to address the court.

"Embedded in Mr Cutler's application before me for the stay of my previous trial orders, was his unattractive contention, which I invited him to correct if I misheard it, to the effect that the trial was a farce. Unsurprisingly, I take exception to his characterisation of me as a Circus Ringmaster and that of the trial I conducted as a farce."

Now, I was waiting for it, but he didn't make any mention of the size of my turds! What kind of legal record was this to leave out such a critical detail?

"Consequently, I have arranged for court security to be present for the remainder of this session," he continued.

Curiosity got the better of me, so I turned slightly, and lo and behold! Just as you might expect, appearing magically as if summoned by a Genie of The Arabian Nights, three security guards emerged, standing slightly behind to my right.

I jerked a thumb toward the gallery, kindly gesturing to the three standing guards that they might want to take a seat with everyone else, as this may take a while.

I predicted that they would refuse my suggestion.

"Mr Cutler, should there be any further interruptions to this court by you, I shall have you escorted away." Justice W. Smallcock said.

"Your Honour, I don't need to be chaperoned," I replied. If you want me to leave, ask me to."

"Do you want me to leave?" I asked, looking derisively at him.

I was a little taken back by Justice W. Smallcock's affable response. "No, Mr Cutler, I don't want you to leave,"

"This case has been a five-year acrimonious dispute." I continued, "You knew this at the commencement of the trial, and yet your court orders are impossible to comply with. According to your order, the Applicant Wife is entitled to a further two million, seven hundred and eighty-seven thousand dollars, in addition to the four hundred and thirty-seven thousand dollars she has already received, and I am left with nothing more than a five hundred- and forty-eight-thousand-dollar debt!"

<u>Dear Reader</u>: outrageous, right? It may sound absurd, but it is the truth.

Julia first filed her application five years earlier. We had been in court for over forty procedural hearings with numerous judges throughout the five years. (You will read more about that in the coming pages.) Despite the continuous delays instigated by Julia, we finally got to the three-day trial in which Justice W. Smallcock was the presiding judge. Julia and I outlined our case. Justice W. Smallcock did not consider the debt associated with the matrimonial asset pool. In other words, according to Smallcock's orders, Julia should get all the assets and more, and I should be left with all the debt.

Naturally I appealed the orders of Judge W. Smallcock. However, even though I submitted my appeal books, which do not make the orders by Judge W. Smallcock inapplicable, my application today was for a ***stay of orders***. A stay of order, <u>Dear Reader</u>, is a ruling by the court to stop or suspend a proceeding or trial temporarily. In my case, until the determination of the appeal by the Full Court. Julia's position was antipodal to mine. Julia was seeking ***enforcement of court orders***. It simply means to make a demand for payment. I was demanding that the court stop everything while they sort out this egregiously unfair order, and she's demanding that the court make me pay up immediately.

"Mr Cutler, there are two applications before me today." began Judge W. Smallcock

"The first is your application for a stay of the orders I pronounced with reasons the day I delivered my judgement. The second is an application by Ms Cutler for enforcement of the same order and a variation of certain aspects of those orders made by the application in a case.

This is where his smile becomes genuine.

"Under the rules that determine applications such as this, filing a notice of appeal does not stay the operation or enforcement of the order appealed from unless otherwise provided for."

Anticipating an unfavourable payback for earlier, I attempt to deflect the inevitable:

"Your Honour, there is no urgency with respect to this matter. In this case, the appeal will be heard barely 21 days from today. If the applicant is vindicated here, then it will only be a matter of a few days delay. However, if the appeal court disagrees with your orders, it may require this case to be heard again or arrive at a different outcome."

"I've read your appeals Index, Mr Cutler. It might fairly be said that the five grounds you base your appeal upon are scattergun at best," and with intent to mock, Justice W. Smallcock continued to read out aloud my five grounds.

"I beg your pardon, your Honour"! I interrupted.

"It is not part of your determination to express and view the likely prospects of my appeal. You have ignored the debts concerning the vehicles, which exceed the amount to be transferred to the applicant wife," I said.

Flustered, Judge W. Smallcock began to backpedal rapidly. His cognitive process for decision-making is now in overdrive.

"Did you mention the debt during trial?" he asked, fishing for an omission on my part.

"Well, of course I did," I answered.

"It was in my affidavit filed and relied upon at trial; I mentioned it in my opening and closing statements. Moreover, you ordered the valuations of those vehicles for the trial!"

I stand there and watched his expression with awe. He'd made a mistake in his haste and arrogance, and he wasn't happy about it. His face reddened with anger and humiliation. Strategically, I stopped talking.

He abruptly took a different tack. "Interestingly, Mr Cutler," he said whilst slowly scratching his chin-.

"Lawyers represented you until the very first day of the commencement of this proceeding, and you have retained solicitors again to prepare the notice of appeal. But you represented yourself during the trial."

He then pauses.

What I think he is trying to imply, <u>Dear Reader,</u> is: -

It's your fuck up, you didn't have lawyers at your trial, and now you're blaming me.

I respond, "I'm sorry, Your Honour. Is that a question? What is your point?"

"It is true that I only had lawyers representing me for the first three procedural hearings and the last two before the trial, but I still don't understand the relevance of your comment."

Apparently, neither did he, because he turned to Julia and asked her for her closing statement.

"Umm...Your Honour," she started.

I was waiting for another tear-jerk Oscar performance, but she seemed to have forgotten her lines. It may have been the brouhaha in the court earlier that scattered her focus, or was she so overwhelmed knowing I could not have been better for her case than that of my own? Julia could easily emote for the courts; her conceit was always masked well before the judge. Whilst we were all waiting for Judge W. Smallcock to return after his fit of rage resulting from my shitty behaviour, her entourage had all but high-fived each other in triumph. I didn't condemn her behaviour; my assessment of how the trial transpired throughout the day would have been comparable to Julia's.

Shitty behaviour isn't some negative "quid pro quo" deal. It's not something we trade or build entitlements to. My behaviour in court was not with intent to harm another. I'm okay with what I did and why, not because it was rooted in obstinacy but because it was a tool in the unrelenting pursuit of justice.

"Your Honour" …she repeated.

"My ex-husband cannot be trusted; he will…"

"Objection, your Honour; that's perjury." I intervened, hoping it would somehow stick and I could continue.

"The applicant is once again making false statements,"

"Mr Cutler, you will have your say. Now, please sit down," said Judge W. Smallcock.

"I am sure he will transfer the assets to another company, either in his or his girlfriend's control." Julia argued.

I jumped straight back up again, this time with a slightly louder voice, once again for increased dramatic effect:

"Objection! 1001 tales yet again! She cannot assert that I will spirit assets out of the control of a company in my control to another!"

Judge W. Smallcock responded by telling us both to sit down. He had apparently heard enough and was ready to deliver his judgment.

Researchers hypothesise that smells can trigger memories. So can music. When people listen to music, it triggers parts of the brain that evoke emotion. I tend to remember music depending on my surroundings or my feelings at a time. Whenever I am anxious, nervous, or depressed, I uncontrollably think of music. Music is my emotional outlet. This stems from my childhood. Back then, whenever I felt excessively emotional, I would crank up the volume of the ghetto blaster and, for a time, retreat into my own safer world.

Just before Smallcock delivered his judgement, one of my favourite lyrics by Stealth—Judgement Day came to mind.

So, strike me down, take me away.
Debts are due, it's time to pay.'
Face what I deserve; here comes judgment day.

"Under the rules that determine applications such as Mr Cutler's, filing a notice of appeal does not stay the operation or enforcement of the order appealed from unless otherwise provided for. Rule 22.11(3) of the Family Law Rules requires an application for a stay to be made, heard, and determined by the judge who made the orders under appeal. Hence, the application is made to me."

"My Order is that the husband's application filed for a stay of the orders is dismissed."

I won't run; the guilt is mine

Too long denying all my crimes

Face what I deserve.

Here comes judgment day.

Julia allowed a look of triumph to sneak through her tear-stained mask, but then Judge Smallcock kept talking.

"Now, turning to Ms Cutler's application for enforcement, the same can be said about her application. The appeal is to be heard in a matter of only days. As far as the application for variation of my orders is concerned, the evidence did not demonstrate to me, to the requisite degree of satisfaction that I needed to obtain, that there was, in fact, the risk for which she complained.

Here comes judgment day.

"For those reasons, I dismiss both the stay and the wife's enforcement applications."

A cacophony of tsk tsk's emanated from Julia's corner. Julia sighed with downhearted dismay. She would have played the perfect Disbelief, Shake My Head, Walkaway parody if it had not been for the total strangers from the gallery approaching me as I walked towards the exit to express their disbelief and show of support.

Their words of support don't offer much comfort. If that son of a bitch could have ruled in Julia's favour, he would have. The fact of the matter is, he couldn't. There was an appeal on foot that was to be heard within days, and the most reasonable practice would be to stay the orders subject to the outcome of that appeal. That's why he could not enforce Julia's application. But his narcissistic personality disorder of being a self-centred, arrogant-thinking, patronising motherfucker, could not allow him to admit he screwed up.

Narcissism comes from having an exaggerated ego; they build walls of indifference and seek status to hide their vulnerability.

I knew Smallcock was a narcissist from the second day of the trial.

After it was announced that the court was in session, Judge W Smallcock barked at his male clerk to go to the female toilets and drag Julia out to the witness box because he didn't appreciate being kept waiting. The protective instinct we were born with helps keep us safe and helps us succeed in life's various endeavours, and the instinct is compelling when it comes to protecting our families. Regardless of why we were in court, I'd shared a life of twenty years with Julia. In different circumstances, in other words, if Julia were still my wife, I would not have hesitated to jump the bar and brown nose his head into his cranial rectos!

In other words, jam his head up his ass!

Judge W. Smallcock did very little family law work before he was appointed to the court. Several senior lawyers publicly scorned the decision to promote Judge W Smallcock from the Federal Circuit Court to the Family Court.

It was no secret that Judge W Smallcock's promotion to Family Court resulted from his connection with the Chief Justice. Judges who are mere finger puppets for politicians and governments tend to sacrifice their self-respect and undermine the rule of law. Some judges resent this, as noted in a recent speech by Justice Murphy-with Chief Justice Alstergren sitting next to him - which shocked attendees.

"Courts must not ever be the playthings of governments,"— Justice Murphy said. "Nor should they be repositories of favours for partisan mates or other political largesse."

I couldn't agree more with Justice Murphy's speech. Judge W Smallcock had made his connection with the Chief Justice no secret. At his swearing-in ceremony, he thanked the Chief Justice "Will Alstergren, a dear friend with whom I have shared many bar adventures over the years."

Appointments of judges should be based on merit, irrespective of favours or favours banked. With appointments based on favouritism, "the seeds for public cynicism that eventually and inevitably undermines the rule of Law will be sowed."

Judge W. Smallcock's incompetence resulted in me paying thirty thousand dollars to get this to appeal. It is common for the costs of appeals to be significantly higher than the cost of the trial. Should the appeal hearing be successful in my favour, the full court will likely rule that a different judge should hear the matter again.

In other words, the whole God damned process starts over from the beginning. All the money spent throughout the five years, forty procedural hearings, and the final trial was basically thrown out the window. Costs of over a hundred thousand dollars in valuation fees, a hundred and fifty thousand dollars in legal fees added to the three hundred thousand dollars I estimate Julia burned through—five hundred and eighty thousand dollars of my hard-earned money was embezzled by the same system that would no doubt incarcerate a person for stealing a fraction of that total.

A senior employee of a large bank once said that by giving a man a gun, he would rob a bank; give the man a bank, and he would rob the world.

If that man were given the bank by authoritative control, similarly, wouldn't "the seeds for public cynicism that eventually and inevitably undermines the rule of Law be sowed?" As a direct action of the Chief Justice banking a favour, appointing Judge W Smallcock— despite his non-existent family law experience to the family court, I was robbed by the system. I did, however, continue to retain my virginity as a divorcee!

CHAPTER 5
FUCK SUICIDE! REVENGE IS BETTER

Suicide is one of the most troubling realities for fathers in divorce cases. Typically, males experience suicide at a rate three times higher than females. Today, in Australia, six men will take their own lives; in America, nine divorced men die by suicide for every divorced woman, and in the UK, 79% of people who commit suicide are male. Of those 79% men who have been divorced, are nine times more likely to commit suicide as compared to divorced women.

Not surprising when you consider the financial turmoil of divorce for men, along with the added grievance of the mothers, usually influencing the children to hate their fathers and continuous badgering from child support agencies.

Courts have traditionally undervalued the strength of paternal-child bonds and thus have underestimated the traumatic effect of severing those bonds through our typical custody arrangements. The courts give preferential consideration to mothers, some of whom openly manipulate the process to become the primary custodial parent. Consequently, mothers tend to end up with more significant financial gain after a divorce and even maintain a level of control over non-custodial fathers' lives. As far as I'm concerned, the frequently used statement that their actions are in the best interests of the child is an abhorrent lie used to restrict fathers from fair and reasonable contact with their children.

Early in my separation from Julia, not only did I consider putting a gun in my mouth "just to see what it feels like," but Julia, being a considerate person and always thinking of others, also taunted me—, suggesting that I kill myself as a favour for everyone during one of our hissy fit phone encounters.

She did not allow me to see my children of course. My first breach of the IVO was when I tagged Julia's Facebook account with an emotional short video of the importance of fatherhood. For this heinous crime, the police arrested me the following day. I was charged and bailed to appear before a Magistrate the following week. Throughout the past five years, I've only seen my children no more than five times. My eldest daughter, Eileen, recently married, and I only found out about it via one of her friend's Instagram pictures of the ceremony. I was devastated! And thoughts of suicide once again came to mind.

I never spanked any of my daughters. The worst form of corporal punishment I ever administered was to tickle them until their stomachs cramped. For truly grave offences, they would have to stay still, and I would lick their cheek. Oh, how they hated that!

I missed the countless goodnight kisses. Once upon a time, I was the Tooth Fairy laying rose petals from the lost tooth on the bedside table to the windowsill. I would take a tiny bite from the cookie and a little sip from the thimble of milk they would leave for the Tooth Fairy, so my children felt that their hospitality was appreciated. I was the Easter Bunny who hid chocolate eggs all over the house. I was even the Golden Book Wizard, leaving Little Golden Book stories on the dressing table for them to find when they woke up in the morning. I never missed a birthday or anniversary and only bought expensive gifts.

They attended the most exclusive private schools, and we arranged for home tutoring as well. I even paid for Eileen's six-month European study adventure whilst she studied law at university.

So, after losing all that, believe me: I know what it's like to be in pain. I know the feeling of what it's like wanting to kill yourself. Julia did her best to bolster that feeling. She unsuccessfully used the children to force me to settle on her terms. The courts ordered a family report "for the child's best interest," but Julia's lawyers managed to delay the assessment indefinitely. Julia even insinuated that I had a drinking and a drug dependency problem in her affidavits. Neither was true, and she knew that. Luckily for me, so did Judge Reinhold. Judge Reinhold firmly cautioned Julia and added that "he was yet to see a child, in all his years as a Judge in the Federal Circuit Court, that benefited by only having a single parent in their lives."

It was a rare setback for her, a battle lost in a war she was winning.

Now, I know you're not here to read an excruciatingly long book so I will keep this short. **Suicide is not a choice.** It occurs when the pain exceeds resources for coping with the pain. People who are depressed and thinking of suicide often feel that the world would be a better place without them, and no one will miss them. After all, who could possibly want to put up with someone who felt so miserable and hopeless?

The contemplation of suicide is a process that eventually leads to a crossroads. This is the crucial point at which a decision must be made. Either get out that gun put it into your mouth, and actually "experience what it feels like," or **FUCK SUICIDE!** Before you pull that trigger, just read a bit further. Let me tell you a story of the ultimate **Revenge** and **Karma.**

My children were significantly influenced not only by their mother but also by Julia's younger sister, Ebrill. Ebrill is prone to excessively emotional performances or reactions. She always loved blowing everything out of proportion because she had some emotional dysfunction and was highly insecure. She made it her sworn duty to make life harder for everyone around her. She was the definition of a drama queen.

Parental alienation is what professionals call it when one parent maliciously turns a child against the other for no good reason. Dr Richard Warshak, a clinical professor of psychiatry at the University of Texas Southwestern Medical Centre, calls it "divorce poison" and has authored a book with the same title.

"The kids hear a steady drumbeat about a parent's flaws and lies that portray the parent as unloving and unworthy of love," explains Warshak.

Essentially, when a child succumbs to the negative influences of one parent, they tend to see the other parent as an enemy or a source of fear. This situation is common in divorce battles.

Ebrill contributed her share of divorce poison by sharing too many details about our marital relationship and the reasons for the breakup with my children. It got so bad that I contacted Ebrill and pleaded with her to stop negatively influencing my relationship with my children.

Not only did she ignore my pleas, but she also actually turned up the volume on the drama and malice.

Her husband, my ex-brother-in-law Yilly, was no better. When Ebrill and Yilly were going through their own marital issues, I bent over backwards to offer them my support. Obviously, neither of them reciprocated. In fact, I later learnt that my ex-brother-in-law Yilly was divulging information about my business and matters of our divorce case to Julia so she could use it against me in the Family Courts.

Thanks for nothing, Yilly.

Revenge is Better!

I cautioned Ebrill to stop spreading her poison and maybe clean up some of the skeletons in her own closet. I was done feeling suicidal and starting to feel a lot more like revenge. My desire to inflict retribution was purely pacifistic, of course. But if I could help dish out a bit of karma, I would surely go for it. I heard vague whispers of Yilly's quirky attraction to the ladies of the night, though I lacked the missing piece to the conundrum, the actual evidence. So, I arranged to meet at a café with an investigator who'de been referred to me by a dependable friend in the surveillance game. I had never needed a private investigator before, so I really didn't know what to expect. When I sat down, a gleaming black Audi R8 with personalised plates was parked in a no-standing zone just a few metres from where I was drinking my afternoon latte. A gorgeous lady with flawless straight jet-black hair, a perfect figure, and legs-to-suit got out of the driver's seat of the R8 and walked over to my table.

"Hi. I'm Zoe," she said. Her eyes were more than just green. They were the kind of verdant, bright spring green that brings back colour to the world after a harsh winter. Adrenaline flooded my system like I was hooked up to an intravenous drip of the stuff, mainlining right into my blood at full pelt.

I invited her to sit in the chair on the opposite side of my table. In books, movies, and television, private investigators are always gun-toting heroes who fight the bad guys, recover the loot, and almost always win the hearts of beautiful women. But Zoe better fit the Hollywood stereotype of the *femme fatale*. We all know the type. She's the female character who preys on men, toying with them for her own purposes. She will flirt and sexually engage the man to achieve his devotion and then kill him.

A young buck waiter literally ran to the table, eager to take Zoe's order:

"Darlings, get me a Grande, decaf, non-fat americano misto, extra hot, no foam," Zoe ordered in a business-like tone that said she had no time for waiters.

I just had to turn to see the young waiter's expression change from beatific to expressionless.

Zoe reached for her Louis Vuitton purse and took out a Montblanc business card holder. "This is my card, darling," she said, offering me one.

Zoe D'Angelo

COUGR SECURITIES

Certificate of Government Receipts

FINANCIAL AND INVESTIGATIVE SERVICES

"You're a Cougar, Zoe?" I asked cheekily.

"A COUGR, darling, is a U.S. Treasury security. It's offered as a synthetic debt security and sold at a discount to its face value. It's risk-free," she explained.

Then she fixed me with a steely look, one that said she was about to go on the prowl and woe betide whoever got in her way.

"Now tell me." she asked, "Who do you want me to screw?"

I stared like she had just produced a rhinoceros from her Louis Vuitton, wondering if she could read my face. I was wearing sunglasses, but not the kind your Grandad wears when he wants to look cool in his old fly-boy jacket; these were more like something you'd find on an astronaut's face. They were utterly shiny, dark silver, and entirely seamless. I could never master the art of the poker face, so sunglasses were the perfect compromise. You can imagine the sparks in my brain trying to connect the dots but instead causing a short circuit.

"My ex-brother-in-law," I replied eventually. I passed her an A4 envelope containing photos of my ex-brother-in-law, his address, car registration and even his work schedule, feeling very much like I was in a James Bond movie.

Being a spy was cool.

However, walking away from that meeting, I felt a sense of regret emerge. There are times when my brain fries up, just like now. It's no excuse, I know; I own my behaviour. In these moments, I am least proud of who I am. Being regretful isn't the same thing as being stupid. As I continue to take steps forward, I foresee a deus ex machina ending. I find confidence, and I find my voice. Damn them! It was either this to teach them a lesson and discourage others or lose my kids forever.

The rule of "eye for an eye" was part of God's Law, which Moses shared with ancient Israel. It simply meant that when dealing justice to wrongdoers, the punishment should fit the crime. On the other hand, karma is what happens to a person as a direct result of their actions. It did not take Zoe long to get photographic evidence of Yilly doing stuff that deserved a nice big karmic kick in the ass.

I could never have anticipated the outcome that culminated from the photos Zoe sent back to me, but I sure knew something would happen.

I sent them to Ebrill with a reminder note to look to the skeletons in her own closet. Complete turmoil broke out within the Julia clan!

Ebrill filed for divorce, and following Julia's battle plan, Ebrill went to the police to apply for a Family Violence Intervention Order against her husband, Yilly. Same bullshit, different family. Ebrill's daughter Rose was barely thirteen years of age at the time. And that's where things get really interesting.

While Ebrill was at the police Station describing how violent Yilly was to her and her children, Rose convinced her auntie Julia to take her to the police as well so she could testify against her father, Yilly. Most pleased with her niece's forward-thinking, Julia praised the thirteen-year-old Rose, and they drove together to the Moonee Ponds Police Station. But things didn't quite go the way they planned. Rose entered the interrogation room, where she found her mother shaking and in tears; Ebrill was presenting a dramatically convincing performance of a woman terrified of her soon-to-be ex-husband, And that's when thirteen-year-old Rose turned to the police and proclaimed on record that her mother was a liar

Dear Reader, if you have never believed in Karma, now is the time to have your hair shaved and the ritual of Namakarana performed!

"My Dad never hit us!" Rose exclaimed. "But you wanna see who did?"

Taking out her mobile phone, Rose showed a video of her mother pulling and dragging her six-year-old brother on the floor by the head, beating the young boy whilst the boy was seen crying, screaming, and kicking in pain and fear. The police were appalled at the contents of the video. They charged Ebrill with a string of offences and called Family Services, who immediately ordered the father, Yilly, to be the sole custodian of the children. It was a stunning turnaround that Ebrill and Julia never saw coming. In point of fact, neither did I. I wish I could have been a fly on that wall!

A divorce can make the best of us act in ways that we might not be proud of. Sending the photos of Yilly's infidelity to Ebrill led to some unexpectedly satisfying revenge, but it definitely took me up another notch on the asshole scale. Of course, Ebrill tipped the scale completely by falsely accusing her husband of family violence, not just for retribution but to get more of the matrimonial asset pool through the family courts. It backfired!

Did Yilly deserve to get caught for screwing around? Sure.

Did Ebrill deserve to get reamed by the system for taking her dramatic performance too far? Hell yes.

But did Rose deserve to have her family torn apart? **FUCK NO!**

Granted, she'd probably saved those videos for just such an opportunity. Still, that A4 envelope that seemed so cool screwed up four lives.

When my therapist thought it might be good for me to start a journal, she probably meant that I should write things privately. Instead, I may have gotten a little drunk and may have posted my grievances with Fat Bertrude on social media and the internet.

It went viral! Oops!

Before you start dreaming up revenge fantasies, think about the consequences of divorce revenge. The temporary relief you will feel after inflicting emotional pain on your ex-spouse is not worth the long-term effects your actions may have on you.

Now that your time isn't spent arguing with your ex, consider putting more time into your career. Many ex-spouses do not like to see their ex-partners do well in their lives, and a few even enjoy seeing you down and out. So get ahead! Protect your Divorce Virginity. Do you want to stick it to your ex and make her skew? Stop caring about where your ex is or what and who your ex is doing; that will be the best revenge ever. Don't bother making your ex your business anymore; Moving on is the best form of revenge and a solid way of achieving a happier life.

Our ideas about manhood mean that asking for help is seen as weak, feminine, or even gay. Don't be afraid to talk; initiating a conversation is essential. Every suicide is a tragedy. Most survivors of suicide go on to live full and rewarding lives.

So, **Fuck Suicide. Take Revenge by bettering yourself!**

CHAPTER 6
IT'S MY BUSINESS!

The pretty Asian girl from behind the counter in the ASIC office carefully reviewed my documents whilst I was struggling to get the image of the pregnant nun out of my head.

"I don't think I need the Statutory Declarations," she finally said.

"Everything seems to be in order; you have the corporate key, completed the 'form 484', and from what I understand, you will be the Director and the holder of both the shares in the company. Is that right, Mr. Cutler?" she asked.

I was tempted to tell her how my access to Internet banking and cards was stopped and to ask how Julia could change the directorship and shareholding without my consent. Should I tell her I have been living in my car parked at a Supermarket carpark for the past three days and haven't showered for almost a week? How would she feel about the police issuing me with an IVO after Julia changed the locks on my home of twenty years? Maybe I've seen too many episodes of Judge Judy; I know that if you're winning, it's best just to shut up.

"Yes, that's right," I replied.

I then received a text from Samantha, my assistant.

> "Julia realised I withdrew the six thousand dollars for you, has cancelled my signatory to the company chequebook, and is now making a scene out in front of the office demanding I unlock the door for her. So that you know."

I immediately replied to Samantha.

> "Whatever you do. Do not let her in!"

The pretty Asian girl from behind the counter continued tapping on her keyboard, oblivious to the showdown about to detonate.

"There is a fee payable, Mr. Cutler. How would you be paying that?" she asked.

My phone chimed with yet another message from Samantha

> "Julia just called the police. They're on their way."

"Cash! I'll pay cash!" I replied to the pretty Asian girl from behind the counter.

"No, I'm sorry, sir, but we don't accept cash", she answered.

Another message from Samantha.

> "Get your shit together quick because it's just hit the fan here!"

"We only accept eftpos or cheques," explained the pretty Asian girl from behind the desk.

"Cheque, I'll pay by cheque," I said quickly, opening my wallet and pulling out a cheque I carry with me for emergencies. Technically, I was no longer an authorised signatory, not even for my personal chequebook. But desperate times call for desperate measures, and the sooner I left here, the quicker I could resolve banking matters.

I passed the cheque over the counter to the pretty Asian girl.

"It won't be much longer," she smiled as she continued to process the payment.

I checked my phone and saw yet another message from Samantha.

> "Julia called Gabby's and my mobile. She just told us both that we were sacked."

I was not surprised that Julia would also get rid of Gabby. Not because Gabby wasn't great at her job but because Gabby and I went to the same high school thirty years prior. She was a keener student than I was, and I was more interested in pursuing my music interests.

(Well, that obviously didn't quite work out how I envisaged, did it?)

I wasn't the flash friend that everyone wanted to copy and be around. I was someone you could run to and cry with until the snot runs down your face, but I was also the one your mother would warn you not to be associated with. My only real achievement in school was mastering the art of getting detention, though I never understood exactly what behaviour warranted detention.

Once, a smug student in home economics cooking class fancied himself a dedicated mixologist and offered me a concoction of dishwashing liquid and Coke. I replied by thumping that student in religious class on the head with a hard-cover Bible and screaming, "INFIDEL!"

It was only my religious blasphemy that warranted detention.

But that was me, and I loved being me.

I would often talk Gabby into doing my homework for me. They say to "*give and not expect to receive*," I thought there was wisdom in those words, but after she felt she'd done more than her share of my homework Gabby stopped seeing it that way. She completely disregarded my prophecy of a day when she would work for me and disavowed our arrangement. In other words, she told me to fuck myself and to do my own homework!

Well, Dear Reader, if you haven't shaved your head by now and still don't believe in Karma, this will surely show you the light.

Twenty years after we graduated, Gabby responded to an online advertisement my HR Manager placed looking for a supervisor in our call centre. Can you imagine Gabby's astonishment and expression when she realised, I was her new boss?

"See, I told you, didn't I?!" I exclaimed, pointing the finger at Gabby, whom I had not seen for many years.

"Oh my God! I thought I'd never see the day; don't tell me this is your business?" Gabby asked, bursting into a loud guffaw.

Ten years on, we both still talk fondly about my high school prophecy and that day. There's history there. So yeah, I wasn't surprised Julia chucked her.

The pretty Asian girl looked back at me after updating her system and processing the payment.

"It's now uploaded in our system, and I strongly suggest you keep your new corporate key secure," she warned me.

Finally! With that, I thanked the pretty Asian girl, took the folder with the company constitution, and clenched it back tightly under my armpit (still smelling strongly of body odour.) Holding tight the new copy of the ASIC register, I ran out of the grey-painted offices, dashed through the courtyard opposite the trendy cafes of Collins Street, and hopped into my SL 500 two-seat convertible.

Driving to the office, my mind was still whirling. Julia had locked me out of my home, stopped my company credit cards, and blocked my access to Internet banking. Before going to the bank to reinstate my access to the accounts, I had one last matter to deal with.

Samantha called and told me the police had arrived. I told Samantha to remain silent and not to answer any questions the police ask her, and that I'd be there soon.

As I drove up to the office warehouse, I saw Julia standing by the front reception door, arms crossed, staring at me. When someone looks at you like that, eyes filled with anger, it hurts, but when that someone has your heart in their hand, it kills. Expecting my arrival, the police immediately approached my car.

"Mr Cutler, my name is Constable Wilson, and by you being here, sir, you are in breach of your intervention order. You are under arrest, Sir," he said.

There was a tightness in my throat. My lungs felt as elastic as old underpants, just sagging instead of contracting for the next breath.

Taking a deep breath, holding up the copy of the ASIC register in my hand, I blared out, "This is my business!"

Constable Wilson read the ASIC register, told me to stay in my car and asked for a check of the document through his police radio. I could see Gabby and Samantha biting their nails to the quick, watching from inside the reception door.

Julia was standing there now, avoiding any eye contact with me. That's almost worse. Whenever Julia stops talking, I know there's a problem. I'd known her for over twenty years, and she had never been capable of silence in a fight.

I recall feeling panicked as a young lad when I realised the cricket ball I'd just smashed was heading straight for the neighbour's window. My panic at this point, outside the warehouse, was different. It wasn't the sort where my balls try and crawl inside my body, and I pace and move around irrationally. It's the sort that comes after the realisation that my hopes and dreams have been swallowed into a void and my existence is absurd. I had always thought we would be together forever, even if our arguments would keep me awake at five a.m. and made me wonder: what am I living for anyway?

Neither of us could have predicted the showdown over who would retain control of the cash cow.

Constable Wilson returned and told me they had asked Julia to leave. This is now a civil matter, they said politely, to be determined in the courts, and no charges would be laid against me for the alleged breach of the Intervention Order. With every second, I felt my blood pressure rise. Just as I was locked out of my home, Julia was now locked out of the business.

Once the police had gone, Samantha and Gabby approached me. None of us had anything to say, and I was not sure at first if they felt sorry for me or sorry for Julia. Gabby was the first to break the silence. "Evan, it's your business. I know how hard this must be for you right now," she said.

I didn't feel the sense of victory that I had envisaged, but rather a relief that I wouldn't need to continue sleeping in the driver's seat of my two-door car, parked in a supermarket carpark.

I called my business banking manager, Steven, and told him that I was coming to see him and that it was important. Sensing my urgency, he made time for me to see him within the hour. I reinstated my access to the company accounts, though critically, and to my later regret, I did not block Julia's.

Dear Reader, considering that the best quarterback is a Monday morning quarterback, I would have immediately stopped all of Julia's cards and access to the company's internet banking if I could do it over. But at the time, I couldn't drop the notion that I was supposed to be the provider to my family. It was just not in me to deprive Julia and my children of a life they were accustomed to. Call me imbecilic; I sure have! It was a very costly mistake.

Separating your finances

Separating your finances before a divorce is as imperative as defending an application for an Interim Intervention order.

The day after I was reinstated as director, I knew that a large payment of just over one hundred thousand dollars was due to be made by one of our largest airline accounts. Though I had not restricted Julia's access to Internet banking, I wasn't completely clueless; as soon as the funds were deposited, I transferred the funds into my personal account, which she could no longer access. None too soon, either. Within seconds of my transfer, Julia called my mobile and berated me with obscenities, the likes of which I have never heard from a female, let alone my wife of twenty years!

When I further inspected past transactions and the account activities, I discovered Julia had transferred seventy-six thousand dollars from the business account into her own when I was in Spain. I didn't know of the transfer at the time. To make matters worse, there was nothing I could do about it, as a conviction for theft between husband and wife cannot be upheld, and I couldn't even contact Julia to ask her to put the funds back into the account without it being a breach of the Intervention Order.

You guessed it: I was screwed.

CHAPTER 7
AMBUSHED

Joe from Pitt, Bull and Associates called for an appointment to see me as soon as Julia's top inner-city law firm filed the initiating application.

Sitting in the outer office blankly staring, yet again, at the sign behind the receptionist with bold silver block lettering, **"Pitt, Bull and Associates"**, waiting for my appointment with Joe, I was crossly picturing Julia with her solicitors in expensive suits and inflated egos, in a tastefully furnished conference room, sipping her coffee out of a Royal Doulton porcelain cup, plotting the death of our marriage. Regardless of how a marriage ends, it's a death. Mine was not a loving euthanasia. It was a violent, one-sided murder. It was a murder, a result of an ambush whilst in Spain, just before my return home. There is more than one kind of ambush; you dot-to-dot thinkers imagine the movie scenes with guns and lots of running. I guess that it would be fun if this book's plot revolved around a woman who was fatally attracted to me, but that is far from being Julia.

Earlier, I mentioned that my stay in Spain was not without incidents. Let me tell you what happened over there.

Five days before my return flight to Australia from Spain, Julia's brother Moey called to invite me to stay with him in his apartment in Madrid. I appreciated the gesture; I happily took him up on his offer and arranged to meet Moey in Madrid the next day. I had a rental car, and Madrid was only three hours from where I was staying. Upon my arrival in Madrid, I called Moey to get more precise directions to his apartment. That's when he told me that he had forgotten I was coming, that he had planned an evening with his girlfriend, and that he would not actually be home until the following day.

Pissed off by his disregard, I called a friend residing in Spain, Jasmine, asking her to book me a hotel for the night in Madrid. It was considerably cheaper to book online, and Jasmine, being a member of an online reservation conglomerate, was entitled to greater discounts with room rates.

That call to Jasmin changed the rest of my life.

Sliding Doors is a 1998 romantic comedy-drama starring Gwyneth Paltrow. The film alternates between two storylines, showing two paths the central character's life could have taken depending on whether she catches a train. Helen Quilley (Gwyneth Paltrow) gets fired from her job, and as she leaves the office building, she rushes for the train but just misses it as the train doors closed; the film then rewinds, and the scene is replayed, except that now she just manages to board the train. The rest of the film alternates between the different storylines resulting from whether she makes the train or not. Jasmine booking the room for me is what Helen Quilley (Gwyneth Paltrow) was by missing the train. My life could have ended up very differently.

I found the hotel Jasmine had booked for me and checked in. My name wasn't on the booking, as the reservation had been made with Jasmine's account, but after Jasmine clarified this with the hotel reservation personnel on the phone, I was all good to settle into my room.

Early the following day, Julia's brother, Moey, called me to tell me he was back home and asked when I thought I could be there. I checked out of the hotel Jasmine had booked online for me, paid for the room charge and incidentals with my debit card and went to stay with Moey in his apartment. The mix-up had been irritating, but I didn't think anything of it. I've always gotten along well with Moey and could never have anticipated what was about to unravel. I knew Moey was kind of shady.

In point of fact, Moey had fled to Spain to escape persecution for defrauding a major bank in Australia. Julia's family were always tight-lipped about it, and I only ever found out about it from a warrant that Julia carelessly left lying on the coffee table at home once. The first two nights at Moey's place were without much incident, but I woke up early on the third day to find Moey already gone. I called his phone, but he didn't answer, so I walked to a nearby café for a late breakfast. Eventually, when he did return my missed calls, I invited him to join me. However, when he arrived, he seemed agitated. He told me he was stressed over a property deal that didn't seem to be working well for him. I offered to lend him money if the problem was monetary related, which he declined. I suggested we walk back to his apartment and go for a leisurely drive, as I still had the rental car for another two days. Walking back from the café, he ran ahead and told me we would meet at his apartment. When I arrived, slightly after him, I went to grab my car charger from the spare room I was staying in so my phone would remain charged, should we need it.

I walked into the room where I was staying in the apartment, but my belongings were gone, and Julia's brother was nowhere in sight. I had no idea what was going on. Just as I was about to call out his name, I was king hit from behind and knocked to the floor. I can't recall how long the beating had continued whilst I was down, but I remember the flash thoughts of Julia's brother being stressed and anxious. Were we being robbed, or was Julia's brother in trouble for an unpaid debt they'd come to collect? I assumed something terrible had already happened to Moey. My temples and occiput were swollen, and every muscle in my body seized up. Unable to move with any grace, my movements were jerky. I kept thinking this shouldn't be the way I go down! I managed to twist and shake myself free to butt the perpetrator's head into the corner of the bedside drawer.

<u>Dear Reader</u>, when I saw my attacker, you could have knocked me over with a feather. Despair overwhelmed me, a heady blackness like a massive storm. My brain was too fried to analyse my options; instinctively, I ran to the kitchen for the butcher's knife lying flat beside the sink. Things had just gotten incomprehensible to the point where grabbing a knife suddenly seemed the most logical option.

What the fuck is with you! I yelled, now pressing the butcher's knife against my attacker's jugular. Moey's jugular. That's right: my brother-in-law had jumped me.

"I did it for my sister!" he exclaimed; eyes wide. My eyes were swollen over, and bloody spit drooled from my slack jaw. This cockroach had ambushed me when I was least expecting it. Now, he was going to blame his actions on my wife? As I firmly pressed the butcher's knife into his throat, he pleaded for me to stop and told me that he could prove he wasn't lying. I gave him the benefit of the doubt, carefully taking his phone out of his side pocket, I told him to call Julia, turn on the speaker phone, and not make it obvious to her that I was listening.

What I heard made no sense. Julia told her brother that she was in an abusive marriage and her life was a misery because of me. Listening to her, I could appreciate why the cockroach thought he was protecting his sister. After I had heard enough, I withdrew the butcher's knife from Moey's throat, and he ended the call. I slowly picked up my phone from the floor and showed Moey a message that Julia had sent me just the night before, telling me how much she loved me and was looking forward to me coming back home. I asked Moey if he ever remembered his sister being abused by me.

"No, but I saw the hotel receipt by the bedside drawer," he protested. You were there with another woman. How do you explain that?"

I looked at the hotel docket he was referring to. The receipt showed Jasmine's and my names on it.

"You semi-illiterate piece of shit! I wasn't sleeping with her! When you left me in the middle of Madrid because you went to screw your girlfriend, Jasmine made the booking for me online under her name, and I paid for the room when I checked out!" I replied.

Moey had assumed that Jasmine and I had stayed in the same room. To this day, I don't understand his reasoning. I mean, he'd left me in the lurch with nowhere to stay while he hooked up with his girlfriend. Did he think Jasmine would be with me while I stayed in his apartment?

He didn't stay around for much longer after he called Julia. The first chance he had, he ran out, leaving me behind, sitting on the floor with my back leaning on the wall spattered with blood from both of us. I sat there for at least an hour before picking up my phone to call Julia. Julia answered just after the second ringtone, which was unusual for her.

"Hi, sweetheart; I miss you so much. You'll be home in a couple of days. I can't wait," she said.

I didn't reply but just listened.

"Hello? Hello, are you there, Evan?" she asked repeatedly.

"Our marriage is over," I said and hung up the phone.

I felt a severe throbbing pain on the sides of my head, a pulsating sensation. It wasn't a typical headache; it was something much more severe, and it made me nauseous. I drove myself to a hospital to be checked. Police arrived within an hour of me being in the hospital since it was obvious that I'd been in a fight, but I refused to make a report. I knew that making a report would lead to criminal consequences, and it wasn't worth the hassle. Not only would it come down to Moey's word against mine, but I also didn't want to be stuck in Spain to give evidence in the courts while the trial progressed at whatever pace Spain's legal system worked.

I sarcastically told the Police that a Eurail had hit me.

They kept me overnight for observation. The following morning, I was discharged and went to settle the bill. The lady at Patient Accounts tried to charge the card I provided her, but the transaction was declined.

"Sir, the train must have damaged the card as it ran over you," she said with a straight face.

I couldn't help smiling just a bit at her wit, though I was now stuck in a hospital in Madrid without access to funds. At the time, it was puzzling to me, though, of course, I now know that this was because Julia had stopped all my credit cards and blocked access to my Internet banking facilities.

So, I called Jasmine again. She was in Paris on a study tour for teachers. Jasmine didn't hesitate to pay for my medical bills; she even offered to pay for my hotel and lent me money for expenses incurred for the remainder of my stay in Madrid. Her name on that hotel receipt had caused a lot of trouble, but it wasn't her fault. She was a good friend then. It was nice to know I still had someone on my side.

The Pitt, Bull and Associates receptionist must have called me thrice before I heard her. "Mr Pitt is ready to see you now," she repeated, clearly irritated.

Joe Pitt had asked me to bring him a copy of the Intervention order that I had been served.

"They hand out these IVOs like they're candy - Is there anything you want to tell me that I don't already know?" he asked.

"Well, I was ambushed and beaten by Julia's brother when I was in Spain. When I returned to Australia, I found the locks had changed at home," I said, continuing to tell Joe all the details of the ambush by Julia's brother.

The story, while so shocking, I could scarcely believe it myself, just caused this experienced divorce lawyer to shake his head in mild disbelief. "I could write a book with the shit I've witnessed with family breakups."

He thought a moment "Is your wife a psychotic nutcase?" he asked

I wasn't sure how to answer that.

"Your ex's solicitors have filed her initiating application in the Federal Circuit Court," Joe continued, handing me a copy.

<u>Dear Reader,</u> Family Court proceedings are commenced using an initiating application form. An initiating application contains details of the matter, including interim and final orders being sought. The applicant is the first person in the relationship to file the initiating application. The respondent is the other partner who files a response to the initiating application. In order of superiority, the Family Court is superior to the Federal Circuit Court, with all matters being heard more quickly in the Federal Circuit Court. When Julia's solicitors first filed for divorce, they filed in the Federal Circuit Court. I didn't know the difference, and it didn't matter to me which of the two courts it was filed in.

Joe advised me, "You need to file a Financial Statement and a response to her initiating application." A financial statement (for property matters) describes an individual's relevant income, expenses, assets, and financial resources. Both parties in a divorce dispute need to disclose their financial status. But I still wanted to avoid that if I could.

"Can't we settle matters without going to court?" I asked.

"Of course!" said the lawyer unconvincingly. "We will certainly try to avoid it, and there will be a mediation session before any formal proceedings in court. But in the interim, you will continue to pay for the house mortgage and child maintenance, and she will probably claim spousal maintenance," he added.

<u>Dear Reader,</u> we have been led to believe from American television and movies that when you get divorced or separated from your partner and earn more income than they do, you will be ordered to pay them alimony so they can continue living the life they have been accustomed to. It seems akin to winning the lottery, as alimony payments are often payable for life (at least on TV). In Australia, spousal maintenance is financial support paid by a party to a marriage to their spouse so they can adequately support themselves. This support can occur after a separation or divorce and is generally limited to a specific time frame. Usually, a spousal maintenance order does not last longer than two years.

Settling things ahead of time can save a lot of hassle. Remember, regardless of how your separation goes down, don't waste your energy on your ex. Assigning blame, defending your actions, and arguing over details no longer matter. Once you enter that courtroom, you don't want to meet the third person you never knew you married. If you and your partner can agree to a **just and equitable settlement** without resorting to the family courts, you are well ahead of those who can't. Once the courts are involved, they assess whether the settlement is just and equitable. Even if you and your spouse consent to orders, a judge can overturn what may have been agreed upon. In my case Judge Smallcock completely fucked it, and I had to appeal!

The court considers all contributions to the relationship and both parties' current and future needs. Contributions are assessed on a case-by-case basis. Financial contributions are all the monetary contributions to the marriage. Wages and the amount of money each person had at the beginning of the relationship must be identified. Nonfinancial contributions are the contributions made that have increased the size of the net asset pool—for example, renovation work on your home that you did yourself. Any work you have undertaken that has increased the value of your home and, ultimately, the net asset pool is considered a non-financial contribution.

You would be surprised to learn how many men do not claim for adjustment in family courts. To assess the worth of the non-financial contribution, the court will look at the value that the contribution has added to the net asset pool and/or the cost of hiring someone to complete the same task. The court also looks at who performed what parenting duties in the relationship. Parenting duties include raising the children, dropping them off at school, doing homework and extracurricular activities and driving them to their weekend sporting activities. I had paid for two cleaners once a week, and I did not know to disclose or discount the amount of domestic contributions provided by Julia, who claimed that it was her responsibility. Then there are the current and future needs your spouse will claim for. The court will consider health, age, and the level of education your spouse has attained.

Do not underestimate your spouse, thinking she will be considerate of you in court. Her solicitors will go after you for every penny that they can. Both solicitors, in turn, will work on billing between thirty and forty percent of the value of your and your spouse's assets.

"If our court date is three weeks away, shouldn't we try to settle?" I asked Joe.

"We don't want and will not go to court, but when we're in court, we need to be prepared," he explained as if this made sense

I felt like someone really needed to either pinch or slap me! Are we going to court, or aren't we?

It reminded me of a scene in the movie Marriage Story, starring Scarlet Johansson as Nichole and Adam Driver as Charlie. Nichole hires a family lawyer despite the couple agreeing to split amicably without resorting to lawyers. He then urges Charlie to get a lawyer, or Nichole will get everything, including full custody of the couple's son. Charlie hires Bert Spitz, a retired family lawyer favouring a civil and conciliatory approach. There is a scene where Bert Spitz comforts Charlie, assuring him that he can't see the matter going to court, but within the same breath, he tells Charlie what to expect when the matter finally gets heard in court.

A leading city family law specialist had prepared and filed Julia's initiating application. The Initiating Application and Response to the Initiating Application must include the final property orders being sought. However, Julia's expensive counsel did not actually outline the final property orders they would seek. Instead, in their initiating application, they asked for the matter to be heard on an urgent basis.

I understood why when they sought a second order to reinstate Julia as director and shareholder of the business and to force me to resign.

If your matter is filed in the Family Court of Australia, the first court date will be a direction hearing or a case conference. If your matter is filed in the Federal Circuit Court, the first date will be known as a mention.

Either way, buckle up for a ride you won't forget.

CHAPTER 8
FIRST DAY IN COURT

"Listen! Stop fucking worrying; nothing is going to happen in a mention"!

You cannot put a monetary value on emotional solace, and Joe Pitt definitely didn't fit the profile of a SNAG. (Sensitive New Age Guy). Though I wasn't exactly asking for a hug of comfort in my time of distress, "stop fucking worrying" was no consolation amid what I thought was about to be the ruin of my life.

Julia arrived with an entourage that would be fitting for Watergate. If the tactic was meant to intimidate me, it worked. It worked so well, in fact, that I regularly needed to piss, and that was before we even walked into the court building. We arranged to meet Joe in the café adjoining the court's main buildings. Julia's arsenal consisted of three senior male solicitors wearing perfectly fitting suits; in addition, two females, one very senior and the other much younger, were waiting just outside the entrance to the Family Court main building. Then there was Julia, her sister Ebrill and her semi-illiterate, fat, ugly friend Bertrude. In my corner, it was just me, Joe Pitt, (albeit not the Perry Mason I would have liked-), and a barrister who was running late.

As my second latte was served, my barrister Rodney walked calmly in, and Joe introduced him. My immediate thought was that I was screwed! Rodney was young and even younger-looking than he was.

"Today is just procedural, Mr Cutler," Rodney said with his boyish face.

"Evan, you must listen to our advice very carefully today," continued Joe Pitt.

Were they prepping me already for what was to be a disastrous outcome by the end of the day?

"Have you seen Julia's counsel?" I asked my legal team.

"Yes," replied Rodney.

"The barrister is Beverley Ripp. She's particularly good at what she does and has years of experience in family law."

I turned to Joe Pitt and asked him sarcastically how Rodney's reply was supposed to make me feel better.

"It's not," he said abruptly, packing his glasses and sheets of paper into his old brown briefcase.

"Now, I've told you every day this last week, and I'm telling you again.

"Stop fucking worrying; nothing is going to happen in a mention."

Having left the café, we walked across the forecourt area to the courthouse and through the revolving doors to the security metal detectors. I emptied my pockets, placing my key pouch, lighter, and twenties cigarette packet into the small plastic tub. Then, I carefully put the tub onto the conveyor belt for the tub and my contents to be scanned. After passing through the detectors, I waited for Rodney and Joe Pitt on the other side, feeling like a lamb ready for slaughter.

Inside the court, there was a plethora of chatter.

Barristers, solicitors, clerks, and litigants were scattered in blotches of small circles throughout the foyer area, probably discussing what would unfold throughout the day specific to their hearings. Then there were the male barristers and lawyers with crossed arms, laughing and talking loudly amongst themselves about shit you would expect to hear after a football game.

Dear Reader, crossed arms hold your feelings in and keep other people out. They show that you've set up roadblocks beyond which no person dares travel. It is little surprise that so many online profiles of these barristers include a photo of themselves with crossed arms. By crossing arms, the message is strong. Don't Fuck with me. I likened the barristers, standing in blotches of small circles amidst themselves in the court foyer, to packs of wolves all asserting their alpha male presence.

An alpha male is a man who takes charge and imposes his will on others. He intimidates, is loud and brash, and doesn't care what anybody thinks. If only a few with wigs realised how ridiculous they looked, considering wigs don't actually need to be worn during civil or family cases. Was it an evolutionary process within their profession to learn to block other people's emotions, a justification to themselves that their innuendo comprises professional behaviour?

An antithesis to their male counterparts, the female lawyers and barristers in their little circles would not show any outspoken emotion but would either nod quietly with acceptance or shake their heads in disagreement. Their facial expressions and body language were easier to read. Is it ironic to them that equal opportunity and the women's liberation movement of the sixties, with the feminists of this movement fighting for equality and liberation from pre-defined roles in our society, now have greater dominance in the family law system?

Joe Pitt and boy barrister Rodney passed through the detectors and led the way to the elevator for the second floor. Joe walked into the courtroom to notify the clerk of our presence and invited me into a small room adjacent to the courtroom. Julia's army was already in the room directly opposite. It was the first time I had seen Julia since she glowered at me in the parking lot outside our warehouse when I transferred the directorship of the business back to me.

Joe and Rodney joined me in the room and tried to explain what would happen when we were called in. They reiterated that I needed to listen to their advice. Each time they said that, it gave me a feeling that I was somehow being conditioned, that after being promised the world, I was about to be given an atlas! The thought of "kissing Joe's ass with grace" was starting to look dreamy and naive.

The Court was about to be in session, and we headed inside. Julia's female barrister, Beverley Ripp, sat behind the bar to the left of the courtroom, and her instructor was on the other side of the bar directly opposite her. Julia and everyone else in her squadron sat behind Beverly Ripp in the Gallery.

The left of the courtroom was quite full and heavy-sided. In contrast, the right side just consisted of my boyish barrister Rodney behind the bar and Joe Pitt sitting opposite him, with only me in the gallery sitting behind Rodney. All the time we were waiting, I wondered as to the cost of her counsel. If my fees with Joe Pitt and my boyish barrister were using most of the twenty-thousand-dollar retainer I had already paid, I wondered if Julia got a better deal.

There were three slow knocks, and I looked around to see who was coming in.

"Silence in Court. All stand; this Honourable Court is now in session," announced the Court Clerk, and I followed along with everybody else in the room.

The Judge entered and walked to his chair. He then bowed, and at that point, everyone else bowed while the Judge sat down—everyone except for me. Nervous as a five-year-old at a boy's Catholic Church orphanage, I ignorantly just plunged my ass back in my seat right away.

"Please be seated", announced the Clerk, and everybody else in court then sat.

Beverly Ripp then stood up and announced that she represented the Applicant Wife, and then my boyish barrister stood up and announced that he represented the Defendant Husband—me.

The Judge then invited Beverly Ripp to outline the case. She explained that the marriage had broken down irretrievably, with no reasonable likelihood of getting back together, and that we had been separated for more than twelve months.

This was no surprise. <u>Dear Reader</u>, Australia's only grounds for divorce are that the marriage has broken down irretrievably. The Family Law Act of 1975 established the principle of no-fault divorce, which means the court does not consider which partner was at fault in the marriage breakdown. In every case, twelve months of separation must be demonstrated before a divorce is granted.

Rodney, my boyish barrister, stood up, said pretty much the same thing as Beverly Ripp, and sat back down. The judge then stood the matter down to reconvene in about three hours to give both sides time for negotiations to agree to consent orders. If we couldn't agree, the judge would make his orders after hearing further evidence from both the counsels.

The clerk announced the next case while we all walked back out of the courtroom, bowing to the court as we left.

I followed Joe Pitt and our boy wonder Rodney back into our room, and Julia's entourage went into the room on the opposite side again.

Joe and Rodney would negotiate with Beverley Ripp and the three solicitors in Julia's entourage for several hours while I waited in a separate room. Each time they agreed to some wording, Joe would come into the room to explain the basis of the orders. The first order read as follows.

1. The Husband shall ensure all payments due in the usual course of business, excluding any salary or payments made to either of the parties, are made as they fall due and shall ensure the Viridian line of credit facility, the mortgage loan, and school fees continue to be paid from the Business account until further Order.

   Joe Pitt and Rodney advised me that I would pay the mortgage payments on our home, school fees, and business expenses before either Julia or I derived a salary from the business. I thought that odd, as I did not intend to pay Julia a salary, considering she had not been involved with the company.

   Considering the second order, it was obvious that her barrister Beverley Ripp's and my understanding of the first order were mutual.

2. The husband will be permitted to withdraw and retain $40,000 (total) from the account's business.

   Julia's counsel had been thorough. Julia's counsel premeditated the order to prevent me from paying myself a wage greater than forty thousand dollars per year from the business. Considering that the annual sum of the mortgage payments of our former home was more than double the amount I could derive as an income, I was reluctant to agree to the terms of the second order. The math did not seem to add for me. But Joe Pitt was adamant that if I disagreed, there was a risk that the judge may reappoint Julia as the director of the business, which would be even worse.

   The third order seemed to be the final nail in my coffin. Even though Joe tried to justify the order, explaining that it was necessary to ensure Julia banked the rental income from the investment properties, I was unconvinced.

3. The husband and wife shall each ensure that all income from the business and investment properties is accounted for and banked in the respective entities' bank accounts.

<u>Dear Reader</u>, your first day in court, referred to as a mention or first return date, will generally deal with urgent matters such as the location and recovery of missing children or an injunction stopping the sale of a property. That's what order four entailed. It prevented both of us from selling assets of the matrimonial pool or depleting monies from accounts.

4. The parties are each and are hereby restrained from depleting, alienating, or encumbering any matrimonial assets, including but not limited to the business's assets or bank accounts, investment properties, and real property in Spain, save in accordance with these Orders.

Sitting in that room for hours while Julia and my solicitors negotiated the terms of our separation. The only emotion I had left was fatigue. Each time Joe would walk back into the conference room to present orders for my consideration, I felt like Moses on Mount Sinai, receiving commandments one at a time from a stern God who was not open to negotiation.

Other Orders, such as obtaining property valuations or engaging a forensic accountant to value the business, were standard orders that could be expected in a mention or first return date. But the next order caused me to voice my frustration to Joe and Rodney.

It allowed Julia to come into my business premises to examine documents pertaining to the business and its activities. When Joe and Rodney presented that order, I took Joe's pen and a blank sheet of paper and reworded the order to read.

5. Each party shall have full access to all documents and information of the entities referred to in paragraphs one hereof, including, but not limited to, all accountancy material, bank statements, and contacts, <u>and each shall sign any authority required to effect that purpose.</u>

Satisfied and smitten with my rewording of the order, I determined it to be non-negotiable. However, I was careful the wording was without punches so as not to arouse cynicism or distrust from Julia's panache team of solicitors.

It was now the end of the day, and I was at the end of my rope. I had just come to the realisation that these Alpha Male clowns in wigs would carve up my future and lifelong work if I just accepted the "system." The future was always something that I had worried about.

I'm unsure if it was because of my lack of wisdom or not having a higher education. Sitting back in the courtroom, waiting for the judge to seal our consent orders, I felt that time had dissolved into itself. The judge agreed to seal our consent orders and further ordered a mediation in six weeks. They scheduled another mention three days following the mediation.

Joe asked me to wait for him again in the conference room adjacent to the courtroom. Julia and her barrister Beverly Ripp had just walked out of the courtroom and didn't notice me, standing only several feet away from the slightly ajar door of the conference room. Beverly Ripp held Julia's hands and congratulated Julia on her triumph. Julia, in return, thanked her barrister; they hugged each other and then walked together down the spiral staircase towards the exit door. I couldn't help but feel pity for Julia.

A week after the engrossed orders from the court were delivered via post, Gabby called my office phone via the intercom to tell me Julia was at the front door demanding to be let into the building. She said that if we refused, she would call the police because we would be in breach of the court's orders. I told Gabby to ignore her and wait until the police arrived.

The police eventually came, and I invited them into my boardroom, where I often conduct important meetings. When I saw the officers, I couldn't believe the coincidence. It was Constables Dyke and Sapphic.

"I remember you," I said, greeting them with disdain.

"Your wife has an order and is entitled to come into your office to examine company documents," began Dyke.

"Oh, has she? Can you show me where it says that in the order?" I asked.

Constable Dyke then handed me the copy of the engrossed orders from the court.

I read out aloud:

> **"Each party shall have full access to all documents and information of the entities."**

"Constable Dyke," I continued with a fierce grin.

"It is my only intent to abide by the Honorable Court Orders. I will be elated to provide my ex-wife with any document she demands - on the proviso that her lawyer emails my lawyer with a list of the documents she desires to possess."

I continue to read the remainder of the order aloud.

"...including, but not limited to, all accountancy material, bank statements, and contacts,

I momentarily paused, then continued to read aloud the remainder of the order slowly—

"... <u>and each shall sign any authority required to effect that purpose.</u>"

"Here officer is the authority I signed and addressed to her solicitor. Similarly, I will only forward the documents she requires to her solicitors' firm once I have written authority from Julia's solicitors requesting the required documents. She cannot enter the building."

I concluded the meeting by opening the boardroom door and wishing them a lovely afternoon.

Once Dyke and Sapphic left, I quickly ran to the surveillance room to see what would happen next outside of the front reception door. Julia, now hysterical, called her solicitor and demanded an explanation.

"So why the hell did I pay you forty thousand dollars for a piece of paper that's worth shit!" she berated them. She ended the call by telling her solicitors that they were fired.

Heavens to Betsy! Did she say forty thousand dollars?

When I took the pen from Joe and reworded Order 5, I knew exactly what Julia and her lawyers were trying to do. Julia wanted access to the business premises to cause havoc and intentional disruption, knowing I couldn't be there simultaneously because of her IVO order. My modifications made it so she could access any document she wanted, but only by going through the proper channels – channels requiring written requests from her solicitors to mine and documents to be shared exclusively through her solicitor's office instead of directly to her. Julia would be prohibited from entering the building, and I would maintain control of the records, preventing her from causing that havoc. I did not realise then that what she paid in fees to her fancy lawyers was suitable for the

Queens Council representation's remuneration, but the knowledge that each request would cost her an arm and a leg was a nice plus.

With a sense of satisfaction, I returned from the surveillance room to my office; I met Gabby in the hallway in the other direction. You should know that I always piped a selection of soothing music in the office throughout the day. Playing a selection of calm, happy or upbeat music in a work environment increased cooperation between team members and improved group decision-making. Just as I approached Gabby, Taylor Swift's Love Story started to play.

> *We were both young when I first saw you.*
>
> *I close my eyes, and the flashback starts.*
>
> *I'm standing there....*

"You know Gabby," I said quietly. "Julia and I weren't always like this...."

CHAPTER 9
LOVE STORY

"The person you think they are."

The late eighties and early nineties were well-known for extreme fashions, such as "big hair," New Wave, Punk Rock, and funk. And who could forget the yuppies lugging around mobile phones the size of small suitcases? The eighties saw the collapse of traditional communism and the end of the Cold War. Microsoft, IBM, Intel, and Apple began to have an impact on all of our lives. Famine in Ethiopia inspired Bob Geldof and Midge Ure to raise money by releasing the song "Do They Know It's Christmas."

In nineteen ninety, we danced around our living rooms as the anti-apartheid leader Nelson Mandela walked to freedom after twenty-seven years in prison.

That's the time period when we came together.

My interest in Julia began when my band played a Christmas gig for students at a popular university. Neither Julia nor I were students at that University. But Julia was there with a group of her friends, and I was the band's guitarist we'd formed in the late eighties. Whether you loved or hated it, you can't deny the iconic status of the mullet haircuts we wore. The mullet was a style staple in the eighties, but it got a bit of an athletic twist in the nineties.

The crowds we played for were often familiar. Being predominantly a wedding band, I would often recognise faces I had seen in other gigs.

Love Story – the one by Andy Williams (Taylor Swift, who was barely a year old then) - was a song in our repertoire that we often played to warm up the crowd.

Playing the lead with…

> *"Where do I begin?*
> *To tell the story of how great love can be.*
> *The sweet love story that is older than the sea.*
> *The simple truth about the love she brings to me.*
> *Where do I start?*

I was fixated on Julia, who was dancing with a girlfriend. With flowing golden curls and her head held high, she waltzed on with an effortless saunter wearing a purple single-piece jumpsuit with the classic eighties-style shoulder. So beautiful was she; it was like the stars were outshone by her piercing hazel eyes, with just a hint of green. For the rest of the set, I unsuccessfully tried to make eye contact with this amazing girl on the dance floor whilst playing my guitar on stage.

After the end of the set, the band walked off the stage to sit at the table set aside for the band. Pouring myself a scotch, I tapped Hugo's shoulder (our drummer), pointing to Julia; I told him she would be the one.

During the break, the guests are served their first course. This is usually when Inconsequential polite conversation takes over. The shift to dance music once a dinner course has been served does not mean everybody immediately gets up to dance. The band is suddenly the centre of attention. I thought now that the band and music would be the focus of the evening, I would indeed have her notice me.

Before getting back on stage, I wet my comb and dragged it through my mullet. Throughout the two-hour set, we played the most popular songs of the nineties. U Can't Touch This by MC Hammer, All I Wanna Do Is Make Love to You, and even Suicide Blonde by INXS didn't seem to faze her. She didn't look even once in my direction. Surely, I thought, if she saw me, she would recognise me.

Dear Reader, without sounding egotistical, vain, and swell-headed, I didn't expect Julia to recognise me because of a distorted perception of my musical ability. I thought she'd know me because we had been childhood friends eleven years before, thanks to my parent's wide circle of friends and acquaintances.

My parents first immigrated to Australia in 1971. I was only two years of age. Typical of most migrants of that era, they worked as labourers for the Ford Motor Company and tried to adapt to their new world. Life was a lot simpler then. They would work hard throughout the week and gather for picnics, BBQs, or weekend family visits on their days off. Their network of similar-minded friends grew rapidly because of such get-togethers. This is how Julia and my parents first met. I remember innocently pushing Julia around on the go-cart I had made as a young boy and accidentally crashing around a sharp bend, then being scolded by her mother when Julia's skirt's hemline tore because it got tangled in the spokes of the go-cart wheel.

"There'll be a day you ask for my daughters' hand in marriage, and I won't allow it," her mother said loudly and assertively. She was half-joking, but she also assumed I had intentionally crashed the cart whilst pushing Julia.

Julia was five back then, and I must have been about nine. Good times. I don't remember seeing her again until the dinner dance night.

Having failed to establish eye contact while performing, I decided a more direct approach was called for. At the end of yet another set, I jumped off the stage and walked over to Julia and her friends' table. Julia wasn't at the table, but I recognised the younger brother of the girl Julia was dancing with and pretended to be pleasantly surprised to see him again after so many years.

My acting was superb; after all, I was motivated by a fabulously pretty girl.

After exchanging a few pleasantries, I asked him about "the girl in the purple jumpsuit." I didn't get much out of him, but he did let slip that she worked in a supermarket in the Glenroy area. Perfect.

So, for the next ten days, I walked in and out of every supermarket in Glenroy, hoping I would find her. I knew she couldn't work during school hours, so I narrowed my search to late afternoons and weekends. Just as I was about to give up, I finally saw her working at the checkout of a large supermarket. It was a Wednesday summer afternoon. She wore a tight, light blue uniform dress, and her hair was clipped up with a large brown shell barrel claw grip.

(Hairclips were another nineties trend. We're talking about exposed bobby pins, beaded snap clips, large claw grips, and barrettes. Remember those?)

Within minutes of spotting her, I was in line behind some other shoppers with a chocolate bar I'd randomly picked off a shelf in front of the register where Julia was working. Julia scanned items for customers and neatly packed them into a supermarket plastic bag. She was a check-out chick.

I didn't mind waiting in line, even though I was the sixth customer. Just so Julia wouldn't perceive me as creepy, in case she saw me staring at her, I kept finding other things to look at in the supermarket.

I watched the man in the deli carve some meat, put aside a slice, and then continue to wrap the rest of the loaf into white paper for the customer. The ice-cream freezer was stacked with chocolate peanut butter, raspberry ripple and my favourite! Golden Gaytime, the ice cream treat on a stick covered in biscuit crumbs. If I had not been in the supermarket under false pretences, I would have returned the chocolate bar I randomly picked off the shelf and exchanged it for the Golden Gaytime. But I was on a mission, and a high-stakes one at that. Even though the air-conditioning within the supermarket kept the temperature extremely comfortable, my nervousness, increased heart rate and racing pulse contributed to my sweaty palms, meaning the chocolate bar started to become soft and mushy.

There was also that perky seasonal music playing in the store. Supermarkets in the nineties were always grey and dull. Back then, pretty much the coolest thing you could buy at a supermarket was Bubble Tape- six feet of weirdly powdery gum rolled into a tape dispenser.

A uniformed guard stood on the other side of the register with little to do—basically an overdressed door greeter. When my turn finally came, I passed the slightly squishy chocolate bar to Julia and took some loose change from my pocket to pay for it.

"" Would that be all?" she asked.

"Ahh, yeah. Thank you," I replied suavely. I then walked outside and around the corner of the supermarket, where I began kicking and punching myself. Could I have been any more laconic? Besides a stupid "ahh, yeah and thank you," I couldn't even bring myself to talk to her.

I could do better. I had to do better. I threw the mushy chocolate bar into the bin and headed back inside. This time I picked up a loaf of bread from the top-left corner of the supermarket and walked towards her register, confident things would improve this time around. I mean, they could hardly have gone worse.

"Oh, that was quick. Back so soon?" she asked.

"Ahh, yeah. I forgot to buy bread," I replied. I passed her the loaf of bread, paid with the remaining loose change in my pocket, and once again walked outside and around the corner of the supermarket without another word, slapping myself to bring me to my senses.

All right: this time, I had to get serious about things. No more freezing like a Kangaroo in headlights! Flustered, I threw the loaf of bread into the bin and approached the supermarket's automatic sliding door. This time, I picked up a litre of milk from the bottom far-right refrigerated aisle and once again waited in line for Julia's register.

Realising I was back in line for the third time, Julia tried not to laugh or smile. Julia had that shy look young women often wear, but it was never morose. Behind her sightly pursed lips was a smile, waiting to be tempted into the open.

"Hi again," she said, greeting me once more.

"Do you remember me? Our parents were family friends years ago." I blurted out. Success! I didn't just talk about the milk.

"Yes, I do. Your name is Evan, right?" she replied.

"Yes, that's me", I answered, feeling my confidence building up.

"How are your parents? Send them my regards, will you?" she continued as she rang up my purchase.

"They're great; what's your home number so I can give it to them? I'm sure they'll be happy to catch up with your parents." I said, instantly wishing for a magical rewind button, feeling overwhelmed and fearing rejection. Even to me, my approach seemed clumsy.

<u>Dear Reader</u>, I didn't have the slightest intention of giving my parents her number so they could reunite with their past friends, and it was obvious that Julia knew this perfectly well.

But she was nervous, and other supermarket customers were waiting behind me in line.

That was probably the only reason she fumbled to find a pen and scrap paper in her drawer, to jot down a number for me quickly, so she wouldn't draw attention to herself and possibly be reprimanded by her supervisor.

It was a start.

For the following two weeks, I'd come home with bags of groceries. I tried not to buy the same things every day, mainly so Julia didn't think I was a stalker, and so Mum wouldn't ask so many questions. However, bringing home bags of groceries daily was very out of character for me. Mum thought I was becoming a born-again son- the son she'd always prayed for but assumed that she'd never actually get. Until, in her own words, I started to contribute to the household and began to "act responsibly."

Julia quickly realised that my visits to her place of work weren't just to buy Mum's groceries. I'd walk in and out every afternoon she was rostered, purchasing a single item. Now, you can imagine how long I would be at that supermarket if I were bringing home bags of groceries!

The phone number she had jotted on that scrap piece of paper was actually her correct home phone number. Mobile phones in the nineties were awfully expensive, and Julia's parents were super-strict, so it wasn't as though I could court her any other way. Regrettably, Julia didn't reciprocate my feelings at the time.

"Evan, you're here every night, and my supervisors keep asking me who you are. I'm sorry, but if you're here again on my next shift, I'll have you thrown out by security," she warned.

"You wouldn't dare…" I challenged her. I refused to believe that all my hard work, my long campaign of inefficient grocery shopping and low-key stalking, had been in vain.

As if to take me up on my challenge, she turned to the uniformed guard, the glorified door greeter standing on the other side of the register with nothing else to do, and I was escorted to the supermarket's front sliding exit door.

I gave up on seeing her, both shattered and heartbroken. (Of course, my new habit of buying Mum her groceries ended equally abruptly.)

I had a lot of free time then. Besides playing weekend gigs, I did little else for work throughout the week. After completing my HSC year, I deferred my tertiary studies within the first three months of starting my course and never returned. Physics and computing were just not my forte, and I had no intention of returning to work as a labourer at the Ford Motor Company's dashboard production line in the plastics plant. Just before that dinner dance, where I saw Julia, my sales position at a Singapore-based Melbourne computer and Panasonic printer distributor had been declared redundant.

The summer of nineteen ninety seemed bleak. The financial excesses of the nineteen eighties had reached such heights that the nineteen ninety recessions seemed inevitable. The nineteen-eighty-nine pilot's dispute was one of the most expensive and dramatic disputes Australia had ever seen.

Overall, it was estimated that it cost the economy more than a billion dollars; it didn't help when Australian Prime Minister Bob Hawke infamously likened the pilots to glorified bus drivers.

While the Christmas decorations were going up and Australia was on the cusp of summer, Paul Keating immortalised the line "This is the recession we had to have" on November 29, 1990. Unemployment was mounting, and every figure on the economic scorecard showed that Australia was in deep shit. Uninspired, with no job to go to or a pretty girl to chat up at the checkout counter, the best thing for me to do in the mornings was to go right back to sleep.

My mother was not the sophist she thought she was. She was apathetic and often overcritical of me, particularly in the late eighties and early nineties. All parents make mistakes with their upbringing, of course. That's normal since there is no perfect parent. But a conversation with my mom was usually an emotional minefield. A toxic parent typically does not treat their children with respect as individuals. They never compromise, take responsibility for their behaviour, or apologise. Almost all toxic parents say they love their children, and the odd thing is they usually also mean it. However, what toxic parents call love rarely comes across as nourishing, comforting, respectful, encouraging, valued, and accepting behaviour.

I recall one of my mother's attempts to give me "the talk" about what constitutes success in a relationship. Her advice may have been accurate, but it had nothing to do with the premises leading up to it.

"Girls are attracted to three things," she told me.

"They are initially either attracted to looks, wisdom or wealth. You're not good-looking or handsome, you dropped out of Uni (there goes wisdom), and it's unlikely you will be successful in anything you do."

Way to go, Mom; great pep talk.

"So, you've got to go with dependability. You must ensure you can provide for your family and treat your future wife respectfully. Always have money in your wallet to provide her with what she needs. She will leave you if you cannot provide it," she warned me.

My mother's deficiency in providing support in my adolescence seeded insecurities, and I found it challenging to create supportive attachments in my latter years. At the root, I worried my relationship would fail because I wasn't as handsome as Tom Cruise (named "sexiest man alive" in People's July 23, 1990, issue) and probably overcompensated in my efforts to succeed financially.

My fear of loneliness and possibly neediness stemmed from the worry that my relationship would fail because I've never really experienced a fully successful one.

CHAPTER 10
DIVORCE AND THE SILVER BULLET

UNDERHANDED DIVORCE TACTICS

"Evan, I need you to deposit twenty-five thousand dollars into trust so I can continue to work for you," Joe Pitt from Pitt, Bull & Associates demanded.

"Your wife apparently sacked her lawyers and now has Shamford Partners representing her."

In hindsight, hiring Shamford Partners would be the most financially devastating decision Julia had ever made. Family courts have always been known as places for dirty tricks, though gutter tactics have reached new lows lately. Unscrupulous divorce lawyers had realised that they can do practically anything with impunity.

They will continue, and their conduct is likely to get worse. Shoddy tactics, resorted to with impunity, result in more victories, more clients, and more fees. Shoddy tactics like the Silver Bullet.

The Silver Bullet tactic is when unscrupulous divorce lawyers, such as Shamford Partners, recommend that their clients make false accusations of abuse about the other parent. It is common for a spouse to get a restraining order against the other without apparent cause. Earlier, I wrote that lies are the messy heart of divorce. The lies can be so significant that lawyers and judges officiate death matches of he-said-she-said. But there is a lie among lies that practically guarantees child custody, optimal parenting time, the money you're sure to deserve-and even the family dog. And you don't need a single shred of evidence to back it up.

Plenty of men, even wealthy and powerful ones, have been on the receiving end of a Bullet like this. For instance, although Johnny Depp is familiar with legal battles, none have been as acrimonious as his split with Amber Heard, who accused Depp of verbal and physical abuse and successfully secured a restraining order against him.

Many rushed to Depp's defence, and his legal team responded aggressively. Depp's legal team alleged that Heard fabricated the allegations to secure a more significant financial settlement from the divorce. In like manner, Angelina Jolie accused her then-husband, Brad Pitt, of criminally abusing their son Maddox on a private jet. Pitt was eventually acquitted, and Depp filed a civil lawsuit against Heard seeking fifty million dollars.

The false allegation of physical or sexual violence is an off-the-shelf divorce hoax so compelling that it nearly always works no matter the odds, hence the nickname. I never came across any father who used this tactic. This metaphoric gun is often in the hands of women. Essentially, many lawyers working within the system use accusations of domestic violence as a tool to destroy their opponents and win the game. Men become collateral damage, and children get used as pawns. As far as I can tell, the only ones who come out ahead are the solicitors.

One forty-year-old Sydney man spent two hundred thousand dollars in legal fees over two years fighting to clear his name from rape and assault allegations made by his estranged wife. He was acquitted of the charges but said he never should have been charged in the first place. High-conflict parents with narcissistic and borderline patterns of behaviour will do anything to win custody and increase their share of the matrimonial asset pool using this silver bullet.

One thing is certain with narcissists: when you separate from them and still have legal property or custody to sort out, they will pathologically lie. Julia didn't just outright accuse me of abuse or neglect, but she strongly framed me as unstable and hard to live with. The narcissist is very capable of telling solicitors, police and the courts exactly whatever lies he or she wants to try to punish you, get the upper hand and win. They project blame, create smear campaigns, play the victim as if he or she has been vilified (especially when things aren't going well for them), and of course, disregard any personal accountability for their unacceptable behaviour.

Once this tactic has hit you, you remember it. Silver Bullet wounds do not heal quickly. Never use it against your former spouse, and always wear a vest. Keep in control of your emotions, and don't react in any adverse manner that your ex-spouse can use against you. If you do, you will be the one supplying the gunpowder, silver bullet, and gun to your ex's solicitors.

Discovery is one of the most talked-about steps in divorce. Discovery aims to ensure you and your partner have access to the same information, and I was about to discover how it could be weaponised. Shamford Partners' tactics differed from those of Julia's previous panache law firm. Shamford Partners used discovery as a tactical tool to exhaust my resources and encourage settlement. By making unnecessarily broad discovery requests or flooding me with voluminous irrelevant documents, withholding relevant documents, and intentionally stalling at every step, Shamford Partners inflated their own fees. They incurred substantial costs for me as well.

Shamford Partners kept delaying the trial by rescheduling court hearings and filing continuous applications for more evidence, inevitably increasing Julia's legal expenses. Oblivious to Shamford Partners' true motive, naively, Julia conformed to adjournments so that I continued to maintain mortgage payments, school fees, and child support.

Delaying and deceptive tactics are commonly used by lawyers, and what you need to be cautious of are the following :

Constantly altering the settlement details and introducing new conditions after the other party has already agreed to the terms.

Disputing trivial items: There's no sense in having your lawyer draft a two-hundred-dollar letter for a fifty-dollar coffee table, but the lawyer is more than happy to do it.

Rewording of consent orders It is essential to understand the nature and effect of the orders you are seeking by consent. When I reworded a consent order to keep Julia out of the business, I ended up shooting myself in the foot when Shamford Partners later drew up consent orders to my detriment. It proved an expensive and unjust order that could have easily been avoided.

Before agreeing that our former marital home would be listed for sale, I agreed to orders based upon a valuation from an "expert" assessor. The order read as follows: -

1. The former marital home be sold forthwith by public auction, and that proceeds of sale be disbursed as follows:
   a. To payment of agent's commission, advertising, and legal expenses.
   b. To payment of all moneys due and owing to Bank so as to fully discharge it and to payment of the Bank mortgage in full regarding the Spain property.
   c. To payments due and owing on repairs to the former Matrimonial property required to affect the sale.
   d. Arrears of school fees ($ circa $20,000) and fees in advance ($ circa $20,000).
   e. $255,000 partial property settlement for the Applicant.
   f. $150,000 partial property settlement for the Respondent.
   g. Balance remaining to trust account of Shamford Partners Solicitors for Wife pending Court Order or settlement.

When the marital home sold for less than the valuation, as per the consent orders, the residual of the sale of the house was dispersed according to how the orders were written. In other words, by the time everything was paid (the agent's commissions and banks, including the mortgage on the property in Spain, repairs to the properties, school fees and Julia), what little remained was paid to me. Julia, in contrast, received her money in full, an amount five times greater than what I had received as payment from the settlement. I may have won the skirmish when I reworded the order to prevent Julia from accessing the business offices; but she undoubtedly won the battle thanks to Shamford Partners representing her. Unfortunately, at this point, war seemed inevitable.

Shamford Partners regularly served me with amended affidavits and applications a day before a court appearance, aware that my response could not be prepared within such a ridiculously brief timeframe. I inevitably declared to the court "a trial by ambush," and a new date would be set. In each instance, further fees were incurred for both Julia and me.

A trial by ambush, in my case, is not the courtroom drama that some of you may be familiar with. The "twist on-screen" usually comes in the form of a surprise witness or the sudden revelation of evidence that the opposing side in a court case is completely unprepared for, rendering them unable to pursue their case. We enjoy this type of courtroom intrigue in television and movies because the main character's cleverness—or that of his lawyer—typically allows this sudden surprise to win the day. It's more fun storytelling when these surprises and twists occur. In reality, this type of surprise virtually never occurs.

Shamford Partners were notorious for either serving an application or affidavit, amending the affidavit a day prior or even seeking leave at trial, forcing the judge to reschedule for another day, and increasing billable hours for preparation and an additional appearance. Do not succumb to these unscrupulous tactics, and make sure you are awarded costs by disclosing to the judge that as a direct result of the actions of your ex's lawyers, and to your detriment, you have been financially disadvantaged.

Fractured Alliances and Divorce Dynamics

Fractured Alliances and Divorce Dynamics. Ending a long-term relationship is challenging, but things can turn downright ugly when outside influences come into play. When people outside the marriage intervene to cause harm, the situation can become even more toxic. This lingering toxicity doesn't fade quickly. Researchers call this phenomenon "divorce clustering", where friends' experiences with divorce significantly impact an individual's likelihood of divorcing. Friends influence divorce rates more than siblings, with people who have divorced friends being 147% more likely to divorce than those with friends in stable marriages.

During a contentious divorce, a spouse often gathers a growing circle of supporters. Hearing only one side of the story told in vivid, exaggerated detail, these friends and relatives generally see the spouse as a victim and rally to their defence. They aim to correct perceived wrongs and protect their friend from further harm. Similarly, an ex-partner's friends can exacerbate the settlement negotiations. As the conflict intensifies and spreads, it often involves both the divorcing couple and people who aren't bound by legal proceedings or court orders.

As a result of this peer pressure, one spouse might make unreasonable demands for support, property division, or even sole custody of the children with limited or no visitation for the other parent. When such unjustified demands arise, the lawyer must recognise this and help the client understand the potential influences driving these demands, ensuring that negotiations remain productive and do not break down.

The underhanded lawyers at Shamford Partners deliberately did not discourage Julia's friend, Fat Bertrude (the ugly one), from interfering in the negotiation attempts. In fact, my initial offer to Julia was nearly four times better than what the Family Court eventually awarded her. But Fat Bertrude negatively influenced Julia by ridiculing almost every aspect of my attempt for a fair and just settlement.

When the forensic accountant determined the value of the business, Fat Bertrude unashamedly interrupted the judge and declared that the business, about which she knew precisely nothing, was worth ten times more than what the court-appointed forensic accountant declared. Peckerhead, Julia's new lawyer and a partner of Shamford Partners, informally joked to me that *"You only get one Julia in your lifetime, and I now have mine."* This line, of course, strikingly resembles Kerry Packer's famous quote, " *You only get one Alan Bond in your lifetime, and I've had mine,"* on the back of a business deal that saw Allan Bond buy the Channel 9 network for $1.05 billion in 1987 and sell it back to Packer for $250 million three years later.

Lodging a caveat on matrimonial real property.

A caveat is a legal notice that enables the caveator (the person who claims a legal or equitable estate or interest in land or property) to lodge a caveat against the owner's property. Divorce lawyers improperly, yet legally more often than not, lodge caveats to provide legal claims to a property in the matrimonial pool. Julia allowed Peckerhead from Shamford Partners to lodge a caveat in lieu of anticipated fees for representation. When Shamford partners then demanded their absurd fees, over one hundred and fifty thousand dollars, Julia was forced to sell the same home she had locked me out of on my return from Spain. In later chapters, I will outline how in more detail how Julia's lawyer, Peckerhead from Shamford Partners, used me to unwittingly facilitate their flimflam practice of taking my hard-earned money from Julia.

Scare Tactics

> *"I learned long ago never to wrestle with a pig. You both get dirty, but the pig likes it." George Bernard Shaw*

Divorce is not fun. It is not a game. It certainly is not easy. Unfortunately, nothing adds difficulty to an already demanding situation like the belligerent, agitating, self-aggrandising bully of a divorce lawyer who happens to represent your spouse. When I started to represent myself, Peckerhead viewed me as "easy picking" because, well, I was. As part of his technique, he always waited until the last minute to serve applications and affidavits or tried to goad me into foolish acts of aggression or non-compliance with required legal procedures. Intimidation by threatening consequences if you don't comply with their wishes is a classic technique lawyers often use.

When the tone of Peckerhead from Scamford Partners got particularly rude, nasty, and exceptionally condescending, I'm not going to deny it; I got kind of worked up. My blood would rush to my head, and I couldn't hold back a fierce grin. The situation often merited my favourite legal response.

"We're going to keep this short and sweet. Do you have a pen and paper? I don't want to send back any letters or emails; I want you to write down my formal response. Are you ready? Good. The formal response to your client is,

'Eat Shit and Go Fuck Yourself.' Did you get all that, or should I repeat it?"

Often, that would catch Peckerhead off guard. He'll quickly ask me why I'm behaving so unprofessionally. I just tell him to "be a courteous professional and pass along the message. Goodbye."

Remember, lawyers do not want to solve your legal problems. Resolving conflicts dries up their billable hours. Instead, they want to encourage as much chaos and destruction as possible. That way, they become more important. Most lawyers have no balls. They aren't businesspeople and are usually unwilling to take even the slightest personal risk. In fact, surprisingly, most lawyers are incredibly uncomfortable about being attacked personally and are not used to it.

It's incredible how, despite a tolerance for causing pain for others, he will usually have an exceptionally low tolerance for pain himself. You actually have a lot of leverage over them by threatening to report them to the Ombudsman or the Legal Services Board and Commissioner. They won't risk anything important on a bluff if you threaten the two things they guard most dearly: their license and their reputation.

Blue Monsters

Disclaimer: No lawyers were harmed while writing this chapter. But a few sanity points were lost.

If you remember the Blue Monster in Monsters Inc., a huge flurry blue Ogre with horns, a tail and purple spots, scaring children but doltish by nature, then you've got a pretty good picture of Peckerhead from Shamford Partners

When I was much younger, my mother would come rushing into my bedroom after I abruptly woke up crying because of a nightmare of being chased by a monster. My mother would tell me that after a busy day scaring people, when a monster enters your bedroom to scare you, you need to scare HIM instead. If he should open the door, and step inside, then you just close the door, lock it, and terrify the living shit out of him until the monster begs you to let him out.

Similarly, a threatening attorney must be made to realise that his life is much better spent intimidating average people. He should want nothing to do with you. You want to be the pig who enjoys getting dirty. When your name is mentioned to him, it should trigger a recurring nightmare and sudden stomach pain.

After paying Joe from Pitt, Bull, and Associates eighty thousand dollars in fees, I was stuck between the hammer and the anvil without funds to continue, So I decided to go with it on my own. Reading the endless email streams between Peckerhead from Shamford Partners and Joe Pitt, I forthwith come to the realisation that Peckerhead, in particular, would write bounteous, imprecise, and disparaging accusations without merit and Joe Pitt replied with contradicting allegations. Both Peckerhead and Joe Pitt increased their billable hours by idly uttering quixotic and dreamy ultimatums, all without any consequence, to each other. It was a performance, one that they both benefited from, that had no bearing on actually resolving our issues.

Representing yourself in family court is challenging but not as difficult as lawyers make it out to be. If your lawyers start acting like the Blue Monster, your first impulse may be to consider changing your lawyer. But this is awfully expensive! Not only will the new lawyer charge you fees to read and familiarise themselves with your case just so they can get up to speed, but your new lawyer may also be likely to delay your trial even further.

People represent themselves in court for varied reasons. Most often, it is because they cannot afford a lawyer. I often motivated myself, knowing nobody understood my case as well as I did. The paperwork was a headache, but I consoled myself with the fact that I only had my case to represent, whilst lawyers would represent many clients simultaneously.

Going to court beforehand, observing similar mentions and even trials, and seeing how things work had eliminated at least part of my stress. Whenever I had the chance, I'd go to the courtrooms of as many judges as possible. Also, to the extent possible, I'd try to find out each judge's background, such as whether they were married or divorced, whether they have children or not, if they served in the military, and so on.

The more I learned about a judge, the better I could understand their rulings and behaviour in a case, allowing me to adapt my strategies and presentation accordingly. For instance, a devoutly religious family court judge might view adultery very harshly, while a judge with multiple marriages might be more indifferent. When possible, I researched the judge extensively. The saying encapsulates this approach,-" Good Lawyers know the law; great lawyers know the judge,"

In contrast, Peckerhead barely knew his way to the courtroom.

I quickly mastered their art of abusive writing. When Peckerhead accused me of misappropriating funds, I immediately sent an email accusing his client of tax evasion. Whenever he tried to convince me that my case was poor, I'd reply with pages-long emails of precedents, including some that I made up. When he sent me notices to admit facts, I would deny the notice, admit to being a direct decedent of Count Dracula, and disclose that my actual age was 436. When Peckerhead issued subpoenas to my financiers to *"produce statements,* **records** *or other items for inspection,"* not only did I cordially comply, but I'd also meticulously prepare and box fifteen thousand pages of copies and include vinyl **records** of Cat Stevens *"Peace Train"* and Rolling Stones single *"Start Me Up"* from the album Tattoo You. Then, I'd return the gesture by subpoenaing Julia's workplace and asking for just about any document conceivable from her employers.

There was a certain sense of freedom I would feel while writing to Peckerhead and representing myself throughout the proceedings. I was no longer financially constrained by how much money I had in Joe Pitts' trust account, nor did I need to make six hundred dollars per hour appointments in advance to have a letter written for Julia to ***cease and desist from damaging and destructive behaviour.***

Initially, Julia was overwhelmed with glee at the fact that I was representing myself. She thought the cat was in the bag and I wouldn't stand a chance against her lawyer. Neither Julia nor her lawyer, Peckerhead, anticipated my determination and willingness to reinvent myself. To be a formidable opponent, I knew I had no choice but to crash course and absorb as much information as possible. Just as you, the reader, are doing right now, I started by reading as many books as possible on divorce. Reaching for a book from your bookshelf is one of the few ways to make things suck a little less — or at the very least, a way to gain some perspective. As James Baldwin once wrote, "You think your pain and your heartbreak are unprecedented in the history of the world, but then you read."

What I found most intriguing was the realisation that so few books about divorce were written by men. Women primarily authored them for women, with the predominant focus on cultivating divorced heroines.

In the classic 1992 feminist sensation *Women Who Run with the Wolves*, Clarissa Pinkola Estes tells us about the wild, wise and ageless presence in the female psyche that gives women power. A generation later, "Women Who Run with Wolves" has returned to a culture fiercely elaborate with primal visions of women's bodies – dripping with blood, coursing with hormones, and pulsing with pain and arousal. Women have come a long way with the feminist movement. The new feminist wave is often accused of having played a role in the recent upsurge in divorce rates. One line of reasoning is that women's liberation leads to a lower commitment toward family, more significant investment in the workplace and inevitably higher divorce rates. Feminism today has found a new stride, a fourth wave. The globalisation of culture fostered by the internet has, in large part, sparked this new wave. The Internet and, in particular, social media have facilitated the creation of a broad, vast community of feminists who use it both for discussion and activism. Social media has made it cool to be a feminist. The Family Court, throughout time, has undoubtedly shifted to favouring better financial terms and child custody towards women as a direct result of this activism. And men, until recently, have allowed themselves to be screwed in the family court and have hidden from the Blue Monster spawned by their silence.

Family law honestly does not know what feminism should mean. From an economic perspective, is it feminist to provide economic favouritism to women in the family court when feminism demands only pure equality of treatment outside of the family court? It is no secret that family courts are commonly considered biased against men, especially when it comes to child custody. Lawyers costume up into the Blue Monster suit to further exasperate the conception.

Peckerhead and Shamford Partners tried this with me.

After receiving email correspondence from Peckerhead demanding consent from him and his firm Shamford Partners every time I wanted to see my youngest daughter, claiming that this was for the safety and best interest of my daughter, I set down to file an Urgent Application for a hearing for full custody amongst other demands I conjured accompanied by a 500-page Affidavit and served it to him the Friday before the Monday hearing. (The ambush practice I learnt from Peckerhead.)

The look on Peckerhead s face, when I delivered the box of court papers prepared and filed by me without representation and approved by the family court for an urgent hearing, was priceless. His mouth was an uncharacteristic grim line amid his stubble. Robotically, his arms rose upward, his eyes almost as still as some billboard poster. His brain seemed to have stuttered momentarily, pausing while his thoughts caught up. Feeling a new warmth to the day, I calmly and slowly placed my hand on Peckerhead's shoulder, saying, "Have a great weekend"

Of course, Peckerhead had no concern for the safety of my daughter during my time with her, just as I knew the court would never allow full custody of my children to me. For him, this insultingly inconvenient procedure was about intimidation, as I was self-represented, and also charging Julia more fees. With my 500-page affidavit, I played their game. When Peckerhead put on the Blue Monster suit and stepped into my bedroom to scare me, I closed the door, locked it, and terrified the shit out of him.

After wishing Peckerhead a great weekend, I continued.

"Hey, can you imagine ?" I asked brightly.

"Here I am, an uneducated, ignorant man. An ignoramus, know-nothing unskilled and, to some extent, in your mind, illiterate benighted and uncultured mother fucker. And here you are, a learned highbrow and intellectual man of Law.

Can you imagine the irony if, at trial, the courts rule in my favour?"

Dear Reader, the definition of "my favour" was anything better than what Peckerhead and Julia were demanding concerning the division of the property and business. The bar was not a high one to reach, and from the look in Peckerhead's eyes, haunted and grim as he stared at that pile of affidavits I'd just dumped on his desk, he knew it.

CHAPTER 11
FIRST DAY IN COURT SELF REPRESENTED

Federal Circuit Court

My first time sitting behind the counsel table, despite my best efforts to appear calm, my anxiety crackled like a rogue DJ spinning torment tracks in my brain, each beat a jolt of unnecessary adrenaline amidst a genuinely painful experience of roiling energy.

It differs from a headache; it's a sharp, aching sensation, more akin to intense sorrow mixed with a paralysing panic that had no escape. Instinctively after entering the courtroom, I took my place to the right of the bench and slowly spread my folders, notes, note pads and pen, meticulously placing every item on the table and then carefully placing other documents that I thought I might need neatly in a pile on the floor beside my chair to my right. Being organised is imperative. Nothing is worse than shuffling through papers when all eyes are on you.

"Apprehensive" was one of my favourite words as a child because I recall once being praised by my teacher for correctly using such a long word. Ironically, it was in the sentence "he felt sick with apprehension"; little did I know that would be a prophecy of about myself 40 years later. I was scared shitless! It's not the fear of when I was a fat kid being bullied at school or of the Blue Monster in my bedroom, nor was it the fear of being the punchline of teenage jokes and taunting laughter of years past. It is the fear that comes from the real possibility of losing my children and everything I worked so hard to attain. The realisation was that my future could easily be determined between the lips of a man about to enter the courtroom to sit on his bench, and it was the sole focus of the whole entourage that had just walked in to convince the judge to do it. I was there alone, with minimal experience in the family court to persuade him otherwise.

I headed to the bathroom and literally spewed. I prayed that neither Peckerhead nor his barrister would unwittingly walk in to have a piss and see my actual state of mind, as it would give them a clear psychological advantage.

Dear Reader, in such a situation, feeling anxious is entirely normal. In a way, your anxiety is a positive sign—it indicates that you understand the gravity of the situation and are not in denial.

When I came back to the courtroom, Julia was gloating with confidence. She had the "I'm Fucking Awesome" demeanour spilling all over. You know the one. It's the "I am going to ensure your balls always remain shrivelled in your pants" type of poise. And why wouldn't she? In her corner was an arsenal of city lawyers, assistants, and overpaid barristers.

Peckerhead settled into his usual place, sitting on the opposite side of the counsel table as the instructor to their barrister, both avoiding any eye contact with me. I think it may have been a tactic tagged to the Blue Monster suit as part of the instruction sheet on how to intimidate best.

There was no sound in the courtroom, yet everyone was moving and whispering into each other's ears. Peckerhead walked back and forth to Julia sitting in the gallery and the barrister behind the bar. The barrister flipped through pages within his folder, then walked over to Peckerhead, whispered something further, and then the three of them stood in a tight circle and continued to whisper within the circle with a half-closed hand covering their lips as they murmured. Their heads were turned slightly to the side depending on where they were placed within their circle. Once all three concurred, they slightly nodded, briefly grinned and then returned to their places.

Within less than a minute, the same pattern would play out again: flipping through pages, walking back and forth, whispers, gathering in a tight circle, more whispers, concurring, nodding, grinning, and then sitting back in their places.

After about the fourth or fifth round, the barrister would break the sequence, raise his head slightly and look towards me. But this time, instead of grinning and concurring, he moved away from the pack and proceeded to my side of the bench.

"Oh, hi, Mr Cutler," he commenced.

"Look, it's obvious the judge will adjourn the matter. With so much material being served on a Friday before today's mention, I think you should consent to an adjournment. It will also give you time to prepare yourself better, as it's evident the Orders you seek are unrealistic."

Dear Reader. *In the 1992 hit movie "A League of Their Own," Tom Hanks's character — a baseball coach for a women's team— famously admonishes a sobbing right fielder by exclaiming, "There's no crying in baseball!"*

Well-meaning mentors in the early years of my attending Master of Business seminars furthered this ethos, prodding a stadium full of intrepid potential entrepreneurs with complex scenarios or first-time business pitfalls with "Fake it till you make it! Show no Fear!" instantly coming to mind. There is no doubt I was petrified in that courtroom.

But I asked, "What part of the Orders I seek seem unrealistic to you, my dear learned friend?" I slowly picked up a copy of my filed Application in a Case while putting on my reading glasses, attempting to imply my composure.

"Nooo…" I said (drawing out the NO).

"I don't agree to an adjournment." I eventually continued.

With that, he turned away and walked back to his side of the bench where his instructor, Peckerhead, was waiting back turned and arms crossed, then leaned towards each other only to continue to repeat the previous pageant. Peckerhead to Julia, then to barrister, then all three joining in a small circle, whispering, nodding and grinning.

"For the matter of Cutler & Cutler, the Federal Circuit Court is now in session."

"Silence In Court. All stand. Judge Reinhold presiding," announced the clerk.

"Good morning, your Honour. I represent the wife, Julia Cutler," announced the barrister.

"Good morning, your Honour. I am the respondent-husband and seek leave to represent myself," I remained standing.

<u>Dear Reader</u>, to seek leave means to ask permission.

"What transpired since our last mention, Mr. Cutler? Where is your counsel?" asked the judge.

"Your Honour, I can no longer afford representation and have no other option but to continue these proceedings self-represented," I meekly answered.

"I see. Mr Cutler, it is not within my scope to offer you any legal advice, but heed what little advice I can give you. At the very least, I strongly suggest you consider appointing a barrister. A slightly sarcastic saying has echoed amongst the chambers of the court's corridors for as long as I can remember. There is no such thing as a good lawyer without a strong barrister," then continued with a mild chuckle, perhaps sensing my anxiety and trying to make me feel more comfortable.

Peckerhead and barrister both smiled and slightly nodded to show agreement with and acknowledgement of the Judge's soft humour.

(In other words, they were sucking up to the judge.)

"I ask your Honour to grant an adjournment," said the barrister. "As your Honour can appreciate, we only just received this ridiculously lengthy affidavit, declaration of facts, by the respondent husband. We certainly need more time to be briefed by my instructor."

"I see," replied the judge neutrally.

Instinctively, after watching countless episodes of "The Practice," the American legal drama about a Boston law firm, I immediately exclaimed," Objection, Your Honour!"

"What is your objection, Mr Cutler?" Asked the Judge.

<u>Dear Reader</u>, Now, there it was. I found myself helplessly transitioning from channelling Bobby Donnell, the sharp head of a high-profile Boston law firm, to embodying the hapless Dennis Denuto from the 1997 Australian film The Castle, fumbling through an argument about an eviction opposing the Constitution's "vibe."

Stuttering, I said, "I object, Your Honour. I object because... because we're all here, and there really is no point in further prolonging these proceedings."

The only thing left for me to say was that "it's not a good vibe" in order to make an utter fool of myself.

I whimpered a little while sitting back on my chair.

But Judge Reinhold turned to Julia's barrister and suggested that he was not totally convinced that there should be any further adjournments.

"I see in Mr Cutler's urgent application and subsequent affidavit a detailed description of the disruption and destructive behaviour the wife continues to instigate, particularly concerning the husband's business. I also want to address the reasons the wife refuses contact between the children and their father. In all my experience with the Family Courts, I have yet to see any child who has benefitted from a parent's absenteeism."

He turned his attention directly to Julia, who had not expected this reaction and seemed stunned.

"Parental absence, Ms Cutler," continued the judge.

"The absence of one or more parents can have a substantial effect on a child's psychology, depending on, for example, their age at separation and the length of time involved. I am particularly concerned about the possible long-term psychological impact this may impose upon the youngest child, currently nine years of age."

<u>Dear Reader</u>, I remembered again Judge Judy's outburst in an old episode when the defendant interrupted her while deliberating her judgment.

"If you are winning, sir! I suggest you just shut up and keep your mouth shut!"

So, I continued to sit, kept my mouth shut, and turned my head towards Julia's entourage, trying not to make my gloating to Judge Reinhold too obvious. I watched Peckerhead quietly compose himself, pick up his phone, and leave the courtroom.

<u>Dear Reader</u>, in military tactics, an indirect approach often involves diverting attention with a smaller force at the front. In contrast, the main force advances stealthily to launch a surprise attack from behind. This strategy, exemplified by the Battle of Chancellorsville, can catch the enemy off guard.

Peckerhead returned within a few minutes, accompanied by several young clerks from his office, each carrying additional folders.

While the Barrister engaged Judge Reinhold with trivial notions to adjourn and dismiss my application entirely, upon receiving the folders from Peckerhead, he immediately launched a blitzkrieg of false accusations of misappropriating funds from the business, claiming I was a threat to my children. He even implied I was involved in alcohol and substance abuse.

"Your Honour, I have evidence of the husband's outrageous and blatant disregard of this court's prior orders. The husband has, contrary to orders, depleted, alienated, and encumbered former marital assets, including but not limited to assets belonging to the business, by transferring high-value vehicles from one company to another. I also have further evidence of the husband's outlandish and extravagant expenditures for his only personal enjoyment."

Excited by the opportunity, Julia couldn't resist adding what she was sure would be the fatal blow. She stood up and blurted…

"I don't trust my husband with my children as I fear he may sexually assault them!"

Dear Reader, Hundreds and thousands of fathers are forcibly removed from their children's lives by a legal system that should be doing the opposite. It has been estimated that at least one million children in Australia do not have a male role model in their lives. This is a mass human rights violation of the children and fathers of Australia.

The rationale used to attempt to justify this injustice is utterly flawed because independent national and international research clearly shows that domestic violence is not a gendered issue and that levels of violence between couples of all sexes in relationships are about equal or slightly greater by females against males or other women. The real reasons for this tragic injustice appear much deeper and more concerning. It is a combination of two powerful but negative forces in Western society that appear to be co-occurring.

Firstly, it is being driven by a women's movement that has been infiltrating society and increasingly seeking to increase their power in a war against men over the last 50 years or so. This has become a very convenient part of that battle – to falsely claim persecution by domestic violence and abuse to justify their persecution of men and children.

Secondly, family law has become a multibillion-dollar "divorce business". Those who stand to gain the most financially from the forced wholesale separation of families are the lawyers, barristers, court systems, judges, police, doctors, counsellors, support workers, prison staff, etc., who have become part of the parasitisation of this injustice. In Australia, this business is estimated to be worth $200 billion annually to the legal fraternity. Urgent reform of Australia's Family Law, local court laws, police domestic violence procedures and a wide range of other measures are needed to address these injustices and human rights violations.

Julia's outburst led to complete silence in the courtroom. What one culture considers a perplexing or awkward pause, others see as a valuable moment of reflection and a sign of respect for the last speaker's words. However, research found that people tend to feel unsettled when silence is extended to four seconds. Even her barrister froze, looking down at the bench before him, embarrassed by Julia's outburst. At the same time, Peckerhead rushed over to Julia and demanded she sit back in her seat, firmly pushing on her shoulder in a downward motion. Her enthusiastic assault on my character was not part of their plan. And after a moment of composure, Judge Reinhold addressed Julia directly.

"There is clearly no evidence, Ms Cutler, of the allegations you have made before me today in this court. Furthermore, no evidence or prior police report is produced before me as to the allegations of sexual misconduct towards the children or misappropriation of funds as per your counsel's argument.

Heed this word of warning.

I will not hesitate to charge you with contempt and significantly reduce your share of the former matrimonial asset pool should you continue to run your case in the manner you have demonstrated before me in this court."

Julia and her enormous entourage were absolutely silent.

"Do you understand Ms Cutler?" Judge Reinhold continued

Every part of me went on pause whilst my thoughts caught up. Shock brings in a quietness within and a moment to feel a gear change for what is to come. It is undoubtedly a signal that a game change is required. It was precisely at this moment that Dr Banner left, and the Hulk walked in.

"Are you fucking serious, Julia!" I exclaimed.

"Yes. Please sit Mr Cutler," calmly demanded Judge Reinhold.

"I think it appropriate I adjourn this matter to say... 2:00 pm?"

There was a hushed mutter throughout the courtroom as everyone tried to digest everything that had happened.

"It will certainly be wise, counsel, Mr Cutler", the judge advised us, "to use this time aptly to see if a mutual resolution through mediation between parties is a possibility. I do not believe that either Mr nor Mrs Cutler are on Forbes's top wealthiest list. I remind them that they should both be very mindful of the significant costs these proceedings will bear and the impact of these costs on the overall former matrimonial pool of assets."

Julia's face suggested that she was starting to realise this truth.

"Case in the Matter of Cutler vs Cutler is adjourned to 2:00 pm."

"All rise," announced the Clerk, and the judge left to the chamber doors to his right.

Judges should foster an atmosphere of professionalism that maintains the dignity of both the bench and the legal profession. Judge(~~Riethmuller~~), sorry, I meant Reinhold treated both Julia's lawyers, barrister and me with civility and personal courtesy, and professionalism, and demonstrated an ability to logically analyse issues, as opposed to the antagonistic fuck Justice W Smallcock who presided during my final trial. I mentioned earlier that Judge W.Smallcock's promotion to the family court resulted from a connection with the Chief Justice—a favour banked. Several senior lawyers were incandescent at the decision, believing Judge Reinhold was assuredly better qualified.

Having seen both men in action, I heartily agree.

The greatest tragedy of the Australian Family Law system is that instead of justice, it is delivering widespread injustice to many thousands and thousands of children, fathers, extended family and also mothers every year in Australia. Julia's outburst accusing me of being a sexual predator is but one example of a legally dysfunctional IVO system in the local courts of Australia. These orders are then used in the Family Court of Australia to make deceptive claims for custody and property settlement under the guise of domestic violence. Judge Reinhold luckily identified the cynicism with which Julia chose to conduct her case.

Standing in the front foyer outside of the court had to be the loneliest I have ever felt. Julia and her entourage walked by me and into one of the meeting rooms allocated as a facility by the Federal Circuit Court for litigants and their counsel to discuss matters relating to their cases privately. I didn't bother going into any of the meeting rooms but just sat waiting in a chair in the main corridor. Sitting in despair, my head resting on both hands, my elbows placed on both knees, I just stared at the pattern on the flooring.

"Evan!"

I looked up. It was my unbelievably appealing private eye, Zoe.

"Evan, darling. How are you?" she continued, dropping her sexy, sophisticated, and undeniably high-end Louis Vuitton onto the cushioned seat beside me.

"Zoe? What a pleasant surprise! Why are you here?" I asked.

Zoe D'Angelo, a black R8 driver, is gorgeous green-eyed, has legs resembling Daisy from Dukes of Hazzard, and has a figure to suit. I had highly doubted I would ever see her again. She had apparently been summoned to give evidence against a case of some Chinese dude faking injury for a worker's compensation claim.

It takes a strange person to become a spy, almost always completely two-faced. There's a reason Bond never bonded to anyone and why the character is such a misogynist. Yet despite thinking this, I wasn't only attracted to Zoe. Still, I had a quirky attraction for what she did—secretly collecting and reporting information on the movements of an enemy or even competitor. Yes. I know what you are thinking. Glorified paparazzi! Whether it's the spy novels I read as a child or the Lotus Esprit underwater car used in a scene of the 1977 007 movies, my childhood infatuation for spy stories had never faded.

Get Smart is an American television series that gained immense popularity in the early 1960s, coinciding with the release of James Bond films. The character Maxwell Smart was created to leverage the widespread appeal of James Bond and Inspector Clouseau, the entertainment icons of that era.

When Agent 99 met Maxwell Smart, also known as Agent 86, she instantly fell in love. For years, she tried to get him to notice her, but for the most part, he refused to treat her as anything but a fellow spy and together, they became, in the Chief's words, "the best working team I've got." Agent 99 once worked as a fashion model and wanted to be a Rockette at an American precision dance company. Zoe D'Angelo certainly had the height, bust, waist and legs to be a fashion model, and I was meagre at best, closer to Maxwell Smart than James Bond, crushing any hope of a chance of starting anything with her.

Peckerhead walked out of the meeting room, briefly glanced at me and Zoe engaging in small talk, then proceeded to walk towards the water fountain located on the other side of the cushioned bench seat.

On his return, he paused and told me he had an offer from Julia to settle.

"Julia is happy to settle today on a 70-30 basis, Mr Cutler."

"Now, this may be best for you before you say anything. If you take it, this whole procedure will end today, and you can continue your business uninterrupted and move on with your lives."

I have twin-track thoughts; they run parallel to one another. One track keeps me safe and is somewhat rational. The idea of all this ending today was an attractive proposal to this track. The other one questions everything, always asking how we could do better. But Zoe jumped in for me before I could answer, and she certainly wasn't shy about it.

"70 – 30!! Oh, come on, Darling! We both know that offer is bullshit.

Stop wasting our time and start behaving. Considering the size of the asset pool, we're not fighting over a house and backyard now, are we? The best she'll get is 55%. We're going to final trial. Now go away. We'll be downstairs having coffee. I'd invite you to join us, but we don't really enjoy your company. However, should you wake up and realise just how ridiculous your offer is, here is my card with my number. Call me only then!"

With that said Zoe slipped her arm into mine and walked me down the nearest stairwell to the café downstairs. With still three hours before we reconvened and bolstered by Zoe's unexpected intervention, I was naively hopeful that a fair and just settlement offer might ensue.

Hah.

MEDIATION

Aside from some time, money and the emotional toll of conflict, one of the key benefits of mediation is the ability to maintain control over the outcome. The role of the mediator is just to facilitate discussion; neither you nor your ex-partner are exposed to a judge's determination. Judges often encourage mediation and sometimes even make orders for mediation sessions with mediators. Mediators are neutral third persons who encourage open communication and help reach an agreement about issues with money, property, or children. It isn't free, but it's definitely quicker and cheaper than going to court.

An agreement reached in mediation is generally not binding unless both partners sign it. Consent Orders that outline the terms agreed upon need to be approved by the Court and engrossed before they are legally binding, which prevents either partner from making a claim later on. Engrossing an Order requires preparing a clean typewritten record in the appropriate format suitable for sealing by the court. Then, it becomes an official part of the written record of the proceedings.

A Consent Order can address parenting arrangements for children and financial matters, such as property division and maintenance. However, a judge does have the authority to reject an agreed-upon consent order. In theory, judges want assurance that both parties fully understand the implications of a consent order before it is approved. Ideally, this assurance comes from both parties having received legal advice. Once the judge is satisfied, the consent order is sealed and becomes a legally binding document.

In my case, Julia wasn't interested in negotiating anything in good faith. She was adamant that it was all for her and crumbs for me. She refused a mediation session unless Peckerhead regulated it, in a place where optimal intimidation could be ensued— namely, the offices of Shamford Partners. Once again, Julia arrived with her usual entourage, fat ugly Bertrude and Julia's sister Ebril.

As you might guess, the mediation was a sham. I was on my own in a room, and, unbelievably, Peckerhead was the acting "neutral third person." It was a case of Hobson's choice, which is the only reason I agreed.

After three frustrating hours, Julia burst into the room where I was sitting, holding a gift I had bought her a year after we had separated.

It was the first time I had spent a day with my youngest daughter since the separation. I took her shopping, and during our trip, my daughter felt guilty that I was only buying gifts for her. She urged me to get something for her two older sisters and mother. I was so proud of her selflessness and thoughtfulness. We spent the entire day choosing out clothes, handbags, iPhones, and jewellery. As for Julia, I picked out the most expensive brooch in Swarovski, hoping it would remind her of the better days when I would shower her with gifts on her birthdays, Valentine's Days, holidays and our anniversaries. I guess it didn't because here, in the dreadful offices of Shamford Partners, I could clearly see that the Swarovski box Julia held appeared to be unopened.

That little stunt addled me a bit. She shoved the impeccably wrapped gift into my chest, accompanied (of course) by a torrent of verbal abuse. I was pretty sure that this was not how mediation was supposed to go, but I was in enemy territory here; Peckerhead just stood and watched. He probably thought it was entertaining.

Later, walking back from Peckerhead's office to my car across the street, I was not in the least concerned that the mediation was obviously a fool's errand. I was too upset by this repudiation of my daughter's generous impulse.

I'm used to disappointment and generally think it's important to keep one's self-respect intact. This wasn't one of those times. I had hoped buying the gift would be a good thing, a small bright spot in the endless dark days of this farce. God knows there were few enough of those. Sitting in my car, I started to cry as I opened the wrapping. Cradling the box in one hand, I opened the lid with my other. I was startled to see a handwritten message on a sticky note on top of the brooch.

"This is all you deserve, you slut! A gift I rejected!"

I was stunned while I worked out what the note meant. Julia had flawlessly unwrapped the package and stuck the note onto the brooch, thinking I would later stoop to below bedrock and regift the brooch to another woman. It was a landmine, a long-term plan to sabotage some future relationship of mine. My self-pity turned quickly into acrimony. Who thinks like this?

The brooch stayed in my office until I eventually gave it to a student employee I knew was struggling to pay for her tertiary studies. I suggested she sell it on eBay. I thought that at least my daughter's nice thoughts would lead to something good for someone.

I have long thought about how remarkable my daughter was on that shopping trip. Sadly, it was the last day I spent with her.

After waiting three hours in the downstairs coffee shop, I was on my sixth cup of coffee with Zoe. Neither Peckerhead nor their barrister had made any effort to approach me with any kind of offer.

1:45 pm, and it was almost time to reconvene.

"Don't settle for anything less than 45% your way," Zoe reminded me.

"Anything less to you is simply fucking unjust! Do you understand me?

Go in that courtroom, and don't let that fucking Peckerhead intimidate you!"

Her eyes were blazing with righteous fury.

"You hear me!?" she emphasized.

I packed my files into my briefcase and took a final sip of my latest double espresso; high and extremely jumpy with caffeine, I proceeded towards the entrance of the revolving door in front of the metal detectors. What happened next, I can only attribute to the overdose of caffeine surging through my veins.

Turning around, I asked Zoe if she would have dinner with me.

Shit. There was an endless pause. I thought I'd just pissed off the one person in the building who seemed to like me.

"Ok, fuck it," she finally said. "We'll have Dinner. Call me when you're out of there."

"For the matter of Cutler & Cutler, the Federal Circuit Court is now readjourned." There is silence in the court—"all stand, Judge Reinhold presiding," announced the clerk.

"Good afternoon," started Judge Reinhold.

"I am indeed hopeful some resolution has been accomplished." He faced Julia's barrister.

"No, Your Honour," replied the barrister. "The parties don't seem to agree on various issues, and a compromise seems very unlikely."

The judge didn't seem surprised. I wondered how often mediation worked in these situations. Not often, was my guess. "Well, let's continue then, shall we?" he replied.

Slowly standing up from my chair, hands trembling from the caffeine rush, I cleared my throat to speak

"Your Honour, if I may, no discussions transpired during the adjournment," I announced, my voice bordering between a whisper and a murmur. My head was throbbing.

Since our separation, nearing 15 months, I have had a single day to see my youngest daughter. Countless requests for additional visits have been ignored or denied by the applicant to these proceedings, my ex-wife Julia's counsel."

I breathed deeply and tried to see if I could get my heart to slow down a little.

Nope. Thrashing around like it was being electrocuted.

"Furthermore," I continued, "the applicant has been highly disruptive towards my staff at my business. Despite my written requests to cease and desist, the applicant continues to harass, intimate, and provoke unrest. The applicant, your honour, does not acknowledge my father as a major shareholder of the property in Catalina used to conduct my business activities. Her claims of accepting the fact that I solely own the Catalina Property in her submitted sworn affidavits to this honourable Court are misleading and deceptive."

As part of my response to the applicant's affidavit, I have included a copy of the original sale contract, a head of agreement between myself and my father, and the bank mortgage transaction history.

I was really hoping the court would see sense here. On paper, Julia claimed to acknowledge the legal reality of things. In reality, she was harassing me nonstop.

The judge flipped through the document I'd handed him.

"Your affidavit is rather large, Mr Cutler. Can you refer me to the relevant page numbers and attachments of your claim?" asked Judge Reinhold

<u>Dear Reader</u>, approximately 150,000 people appear in family court each year. It is estimated that between 30% and 40% of these cases involve a party who is self-represented at some point during the process. This means that 45,000 to 60000 individuals navigate the system on their own. Despite the challenges, they all make it through, though with varying degrees of success.

If both sides represent themselves, then the odds of winning are fifty-fifty. However, in cases where one side has a lawyer, and the other doesn't, the self-rep does way worse. There are many reasons for this, but we will focus on the best way to improve those odds.

You need to organise your material and whatever exhibits you may need to tell your story to a judge sensibly. For your written material, tell your story in a way that makes sense, reads naturally, and puts the important things the judge needs to know upfront and effortlessly. Use headings and subheadings to clarify your content and include any exhibits you need. When referring to your material, use colour tabs and labels so you don't have to shuffle through bundles of folders and papers in court, possibly irritating the judge and making you nervous.

This time, I was ready. "Your Honour, please refer to attachment seven, page twelve; attachment eleven, page twenty-one; and attachment fourteen, page thirty-six."

"Very good. Please continue Mr Cutler," continued Judge Reinhold.

"Your Honour, I have provided fifteen thousand pages of evidence that were asked of me. To date, the applicant has not been truthful and continues to ignore my request for disclosure and further and better particulars."

<u>Dear Reader</u>, the duty of disclosure is the requirement that a person be transparent about their circumstances and disclose all relevant information and documents related to issues in dispute to the other party and the court in the course of family law proceedings. This duty applies to both parenting and financial matters. I had done so at excruciating length. Julia, with the collusion of her legal personal entourage, had not.

"Your Honour", I continued.

The applicant wife continues to mislead this honourable court and refuses to disclose her actual state of employment. I seek leave Your Honour to subpoena her place of employment.

For once, the universe didn't kick me in the shins for the fun of it.

"Mr Cutler. I find it appropriate to include leave for the husband to issue a subpoena within my orders today. Are there any further matters you wish to raise before this court today?"

"No, thank you, your honour," I replied and just dropped like a heap of shit back onto my chair.

Dear Reader, there's obviously a lot more that I could have said about Julia. I could have reminded the Judge how Julia accused me of being sexually abusive towards my daughters, for example. But I didn't. Forget the nasty. As tempting as it is to tell the judge how nasty the other person is so they'll know the real her, forget it. Judges don't like mud thrown around. Even if it's true, it weakens your argument. Stick to the essential things: what is best for your children. That makes your presentation much more effective. And when you absolutely have to say something bad about the other person, do it in a way that shows how it affects your children or their credibility. Don't make it about yourself. Make it about whatever the judge has to deal with. Trying to make the judge feel sympathetic to you and your woes just isn't a good strategy, even though it may feel good.

"Counsel for the applicant wife," continued Judge Reinhold. And now it was time for Julia's team to try and screw me over some more.

"Thank you, your honour," Julia's barrister replied.

"Contrary to orders, the Defendant Husband, Mr Cutler, has depleted, alienated, and encumbered former marital assets, including but not limited to assets belonging to the business, by transferring high-value vehicles from one company to another. The husband has also sustained and enjoyed extravagant expenditures for his own enjoyment. We seek to hold the company liable and pay my client a sum equal to these expenditures, as my client can barely put food on her table for herself and her children." He said this with a straight face, sitting at a table with a team of high-priced lawyers who were surely just helping Julia out of the goodness of their hearts.

The judge wasn't buying it... Also, he caught what they were trying to do.

"Surely, Counsel, you are not proposing that the company pay your client an equal proportion of its fixed costs?" asked Judge Reinhold

"Ahh, no, your Honour," the barrister back-pedalled.

Dear Reader, They were trying to sneak through some bald-faced robbery through clever wording. Asking the judge to award Julia a value equal to the business expenditures would put the business in massive debt to Julia. At the time, I didn't fully appreciate the underlying and detrimental consequences that could have transpired if Judge Reinhold's astuteness had not prevailed. But Julia's team wasn't ready to concede this point so readily.

"Your honour," continued the Barrister.

"It's prudent to appoint an administrator to the business as the husband continues to deplete its cash reserve and assets."

"Counsel, I am not prepared to incur substantial and unnecessary costs to the business," replied Judge Reinhold.

"Mr. Cutler, can you confirm that the business's fixed operating costs are paid, the company remains liquid, and it can meet its obligatory costs?"

"Your Honour," I replied as I stood up.

"The business has always remained solvent. I have included affidavits from my staff and evidence of the applicant's interference, including her contacting my financiers and advising them that the business is bankrupt and that I have fled to Spain. This has caused my financier's significant hesitation to continue supporting my business. However, the company remains solvent regardless."

The Judge nodded "At this stage, I am not prepared to set orders that will undermine the business's ability to continue to trade." he said. "Further, I note that Mr Cutler is self-represented due to the depletion of available funds to pay further legal costs, whereby your client enjoys representation."

Dear Reader, most of what happened at this stage passed right over my head. At the time, I didn't realise that Julia's counsel was, in fact, laying the groundwork to force the business to liquidate!

"I am ready to announce my orders," Judge Reinhold finally continued. And this is what he said.

"Order 1. The Respondent's father, Mr Cutler Senior, will be joined as an intervenor."

"Order 2. Mr Cutler has leave to subpoena the applicant wife's place of employment, bank statements, and all further documents the defendant husband deems necessary for the purpose of disclosure."

"Order 3. Family Report. Solicitors for the applicant shall forthwith arrange the earliest possible Family Report and request that it be made available prior to 27 August 2015."

"Order 4. The parties' solicitors (or if they are unrepresented, the partiers themselves) shall send to the other and the nominated mediator, at least seven days before the mediation, copies of:

a. Written confirmation by each party or their solicitors that:

(i) All relevant documents have been exchanged between the parties; and

(ii) The superannuation trustee of any fund that may be the subject of a splitting order has been accorded procedural fairness.

b. An outline of the case document in the form set out below in the trial directions.

c. A copy of a market appraisal or valuations of any asset or financial resource, the value of which is disputed and valuations of any superannuation interests.

d. A copy of the actual terms of orders required to give effect to their settlement proposal.

The court further orders all outstanding applications be adjourned to 28 August 2015 at noon for an interim hearing."

I couldn't believe it. Had the judge actually done what I asked?

"All rise," announced the clerk.

The matter for Cutler vs Cutler is now adjourned.

Gripping the arms of my chair tightly, I looked towards the left of me and noticed nobody from Julia's counsel was looking back in my direction. They certainly weren't smiling or congratulating one another. No smug, condescending looks or scornful glares. Quietly, they gathered their folders, turned around, and left the courtroom, tails between their legs. Did I just win? I asked myself.

It's not that simple. Because people see the truth from different perspectives, their narratives of the same events are often entirely different. Your mind experiences confusion when your conscious brain can't process things, but your subconscious can. Clarity didn't come until the courtroom was completely vacated.

A reasonable compromise is always better than a fight-to-the-death victory. We generally don't like to settle for less if we feel certain things are the "right" conclusion. In Julia's case, her friends and family encouraged her to "keep up the fight." But a settlement in a family court case is more often than not the wisest and most effective thing you can do.

First, you never really know what the judge will do. Just because you're sure you should win doesn't mean you can be sure you will win. Even experienced lawyers sometimes lose cases they thought were sure to win. I offered Julia one million three hundred thousand dollars and would have negotiated further. But Julia demanded five million dollars. The problem was that our total asset pool was nowhere near the value that she demanded. The five-million-dollar figure was based upon Julia's friend Fat Bertrude telling her the business was worth far more than it was.

Don't count on getting all you want if you leave it to a judge to decide. Peckerhead truly underestimated my ability to research and reinvent myself. Getting the information you need is complex, especially if you're representing yourself, but there are ways.

Search the internet for information, but be careful. You need to be sure that what you're looking at is dependable and valuable. Know what you're talking about. Making sure you know what your request is about allows you to answer questions from the judge straightforwardly. You'll have a better idea about what makes a reasonable compromise. And you will have a more sensible set of expectations about how your matter will end.

After the first day of representing myself, my confidence was hard-won yet deep, purging that which was born of fear; I felt like a phoenix, one who has suffered and been reduced to ashes and then reborn. I had metamorphosed from that timid first day of self-representation; it was a stark contrast with my experience with Judge Small Cock.

Dinner at Vue de Monde

You've seen those photographs where the background is blurred, and the only part in focus is the person at the centre of the picture. That was Zoe walking into Vue de Monde, the restaurant where we met. Every other detail of that place blurred as every part of me focussed on every aspect of her. She walked without shame or false modesty, knowing she was beautiful. Sleek with an athletic frame, Zoe had the breasts of a French actress. Small-chested women glanced her way in envy—they knew they were outdone. Looks aren't everything, and love, it would seem, is far from blind. Across cultures and sexes, some features hold greater appeal. Symmetrical faces emerge as universally attractive (sorry, Picasso), and being fit and having a bit of muscle go a long way in sexual attraction.

My attraction to Zoe was the sanest kind of madness.

Ah, madness, that delightful state where reason takes a vacation, tips generously, and leaves you with the bill. Picture this: you wake up in the morning and decide to floss with spaghetti instead of brushing your teeth. Because why not? Dental hygiene is so passe, really; who needs minty freshness? Madness is when you're convinced that your neighbour's pet goldfish is plotting world domination. You know that little orange swimmer with beady eyes? It probably secretly drafts treaties with rats and forms alliances with pigeons. Soon, it'll demand a seat in the United Nations. But wait, there's more! Madness is when you decide to organise your sock drawer by existential dread levels.

The fluffy ones? Existential crisis level: mild.

The mismatched ones? Existential, crisis level: moderate.

And that lone sock without a partner? Existential crisis level: DEFCON 1.

Albert Einstein once defined madness as "repeating the same action, over and over, hoping for a different result." Madness over your sock drawer is a minor problem, but the madness of family court litigation is another matter. It persists every day because divorced couples cannot get along and cooperate just enough to do a sensible out-of-court settlement that is reasonably fair for both and their children. I recently read in the newspaper that one divorcing couple spent 1.1 million dollars in legal fees fighting over property worth only about 1.8 million. This seems like the definition of madness to me.

And the unethical, unscrupulous, bottom-feeding lawyers converging to extract money from the carnage are part of the problem. The madness of how simple and cheap (minus the wedding) it is to get married and how complicated and expensive it is to get divorced is akin to how both partners are presented as high-functioning and bring with them stories of happy beginnings and miserable endings. The courtroom becomes a stage for dramatically unravelling relationships, where love once bloomed but now festers in bitterness. The madness of the whole process propels people to dysfunctional states that profit no one but the lawyers. It's akin to a temporary form of insanity that arises during the divorce itself and lingers within the ex-romantic relationship like an invisible, toxic mist. This mist distorts reality, hinders healthy impulses, and amplifies pre-existing character flaws. You meet the third person you married. The person they're going to become in the family court.

The madness of legal costs can be especially bewildering and exasperating. Legal representation during divorce proceedings comes at a hefty price. Lawyers charge by the hour, and their fees can escalate rapidly. The meter ticks relentlessly as they draft documents, attend hearings, and engage in negotiations. It's not generally money well-spent. It is not uncommon for lawyers themselves to engage in serious misconduct, such as frivolous actions, dishonesty, or malicious conduct. In these scenarios, the madness of divorce costs becomes painfully evident.

That kind of madness detracts from life. What I was experiencing in this restaurant as Zoe walked in was entirely different.

Vue de Monde's dining room is a canvas of muted tones— soft greys, velvety blues, and burnished gold. Tables, spaced discreetly, boast crisp white linens. Crystal stemware catches the light, and silver flatware gleams. As you settle into your chair, the city unfolds below in a tapestry of lights and life. The ceiling, a celestial map, twinkles with constellations. The hushed murmur of fellow diners only adds to the ambience. And if you're sitting with someone straight out of a Bond movie, it's even more unreal.

"They're absolutely bonkers, Evan!" Zoe's exclamation echoed through the posh restaurant as the waiter guided her to the table. The ambience in Vue de Monde seemed to amplify her frustration.

I could only listen and agree. "Evan, my brother, Vince, and his ex-wife had just finalised their own divorce in Brisbane. Their combined net assets totalled a staggering 1.5 million dollars. You'd think a rational person would accept a fair settlement, right? Well, not her.

The proposed split was already leaning in her favour — 65% to her, 35% to my brother. But instead of gracefully accepting the offer, Vince's ex embarked on a wild legal spending spree. Picture this: she hired a lawyer who charged more per hour than a private jet rental. And what did she achieve with this pricey legal circus? The same fucking damn settlement she had initially rejected!

It's like watching a courtroom drama scripted by Dr Seuss. The judge must have been wondering if he'd accidentally wandered into a whimsical parallel universe. Perhaps their court stenographer was typing out rhymes instead of legal jargon:

Your Honor, I present Exhibit A: Green Eggs and Child Support. The applicant claims she deserves the golden goose, but the defendant husband argues that the goose is actually a platypus in disguise." Madness.

As Zoe settled into her chair, she shot me a look, "Welcome to the circus darling." she said. And we raised our glasses to the absurdity of it all.

Because sometimes life's plot twists are more nonsensical than a cat in the hat.

(Disclaimer: No goldfish were harmed in the making of this chapter. But their ambitions remain suspect.)

CHAPTER 12
PSYCHOLOGY OF DIVORCE

Why the hell do people put themselves through all this?

Dear Reader, in this exploration of the psychology of divorce, let's delve into the emotional currents, the factors that predispose some couples to separation, and the transformative potential that emerges from the shit left behind after a broken marriage. Whether it's conscious uncoupling or the tumultuous aftermath, divorce leaves an indelible mark on your psyche. By the end of this chapter, you will convince yourself that this story was written about you and describes how you ended up where you are today with uncanny accuracy.

The emotional landscape of divorce is a rollercoaster of grief, anger, relief, and anxiety. You grapple with questions of identity, loss, and personal growth. A cascade of expected and unexpected psychological responses was unleashed when your marriage unravelled.

The courtroom drama is only part of the story of course. While a legal divorce is a formal event that occurs when a judge signs a marital dissolution decree, an emotional divorce is better understood as a gradual process; it unfolds over several years and can even extend throughout a person's lifetime. Typically, the emotional divorce begins well before the actual separation date. During this period, one of the spouses generally experiences a predictable range of emotions, including disillusionment, dissatisfaction, anxiety, and alienation.

Divorce research indicates that in 75 to 90 per cent of contemporary divorces, one spouse desires to end the marriage while the other does not. Interestingly, women tend to initiate divorce more frequently. The lack of mutual agreement regarding divorce decisions significantly impacts the divorce process. The spouse who initiates the emotional separation often starts this journey years before the other partner, leading to disagreements that bring everyone to court.

You are now about to meet the third person you married.

The person they're now going to become in the family court.

By the time legal divorce proceedings begin, one spouse may be emotionally prepared, while the other may just have learned about the impending physical separation. Consequently, a substantial discrepancy exists in your emotional status when it's time to see lawyers.

Many divorce researchers view the process as a sequence of developmental phases that divorcing families navigate. Although these stages are typically seen as linear, they are not rigidly fixed. Some couples may skip stages or experience feelings and behaviours from multiple stages simultaneously. The intensity of progression through these stages varies, influenced by the couple's ambivalence toward the divorce. Nonetheless, different models and these stages exhibit similar characteristic patterns.

Typically, a woman facing marital stress employs various coping mechanisms before deciding to separate or divorce. These strategies range from expressing anger and confrontation with her spouse in the hope of inducing change to withdrawing emotionally to avoid the pain of communication breakdown. She might immerse herself in work, spend excessive time with friends, or even resort to extramarital affairs, substance use, or (in extreme cases) of physical or verbal abuse. If one of these tactics yields results, and her husband refuses counselling, or counselling proves ineffective in alleviating her feelings of despair, she may ultimately choose divorce. At this juncture, a sense of inevitability often sets in – a moment when the wife emotionally detaches from the marriage. Left with no other recourse, she announces her desire for separation. This declaration triggers the husband's initial response, which may include denial or emotional withdrawal as a form of self-protection.

When faced with the reality that denial no longer shields him from the situation, the husband grapples with his own whirlwind of emotions: anguish, shock, and disbelief. Initially, he may feign normalcy, even if his wife consistently rejects his attempts. This denial gives rise to a separate rollercoaster of reactions: anger, a desire to bargain, and confusion, all in an effort to regain some semblance of control. Seeking guidance, he often turns to friends and family, seeking advice on how to win her back. He may also reach out to therapists, scheduling one appointment after another in the hope that a professional can persuade her to reconsider leaving the marriage.

The husband usually interprets his wife's actions as a momentary upset (or insanity,) a mid-life crisis, or a premature surrender. He rarely grants her the opportunity to prove herself. If these justifications fail, he might confess to all his perceived shortcomings and agree to participate in thorough individual and couples counselling, committing to reforming his behaviour, hoping to convince her of his desire to reconcile. However, the wife generally asserts that it's already too late. Emotionally, she made her decision long before counselling began, and these efforts on the husband's part serve more as a formality and face-saving measure. In cases where the husband really struggles to accept the impending divorce, the wife may request that the therapist focus solely on him, aiding him through this challenging period. But the husband's real goal in therapy is usually to save the marriage, a strategic approach that becomes evident when he eventually drops out after failing to win his wife's affection in the marriage through his self-improvement.

Overwhelmed and desperate, the husband might, at this point, resort to making threats: withholding access to the children, refusing financial support, or claiming ownership of the house, business, and all assets. He may even try to intimidate her by suggesting she cannot survive financially without him. When these threats fail, his self-pity sometimes drives him to the brink of attempting suicide. Typically, he orchestrates this in a manipulative manner, ensuring someone (often the wife) is aware of his actions; in reality, he usually isn't interested in genuinely risking his life but in making a powerful and desperate statement. Despite his intense panic, his survival instinct ultimately prevails.

ANGER

Often expressed through various threats, this is typically a secondary emotion. In other words, it masks deeper primary feelings such as hurt, fear, humiliation, loss, abandonment, and a sense of powerlessness. Unfortunately, professionals involved in divorce cases sometimes misinterpret the husband's threats as evidence of violent tendencies rather than recognising them as understandable reactions to a complex mix of emotions. Anger can serve a protective function, shielding an individual from the intense psychological trauma associated with a separating partner. Divorce and marital separation, in fact, rank as the second and third most significant life stressors someone is likely to experience, following only the death of a spouse.

During the legal divorce or litigation stage

During the legal divorce or litigation stage, the husband may seek legal counsel when none of the previous actions alleviates his feelings of helplessness and confusion. His decision to do so may either be in response to his wife having already filed for divorce or as a pre-emptive move to file before she does. It's essential to recognise that the initiator of the divorce isn't always the one who files first. Sometimes, the spouse being left behind initiates the process of maintaining a semblance of control amidst the emotional turmoil. Alternatively, it may be a final attempt to jolt the other partner into awareness by presenting the logical consequences of their emotionally detached behaviour. In some cases, it becomes a retaliatory act fuelled by anger— a variation of "You can't fire me because I fucking quit!" This marks the beginning of the litigation phase for a legal divorce, during which the various leeches, including attorneys, accountants, real estate appraisers, therapists, mediators, and evaluators, begin to suck the blood from the divorcing couple.

Following the physical separation and the initiation of legal divorce proceedings

Following the physical separation and the initiation of legal divorce proceedings, the wife, on her part, encounters a range of emotions. These include feelings of relief, confusion, loneliness, and sadness. Her ambivalence about the separation often leads her to oscillate between these emotions and others. One particular complex feeling that emerges from this mixture is guilt. This guilt often correlates with the extent of hurt expressed or demonstrated by her husband. Guilt and hurt operate in tandem— as one intensifies, so does the other, and vice versa. The wife's guilt may stem from concerns about disrupting the family unit, leaving her husband in distress and depression, impacting the children's psychological well-being, and more. Her guilt amplifies when her husband displays vulnerability, sadness, and daily dysfunction. She may even question her decision to leave and contemplate reuniting to alleviate his pain and her loneliness.

However, she will not consider relinquishing her rights to an equitable division of property and a fair support plan.

In cases of separation, if the husband reacts with anger, bitterness and vindictiveness, the wife's feelings of guilt often take a back seat to defensiveness, withdrawal, and detachment. She might perceive him as an aggressive and potentially dangerous person, especially concerning their children, and if so, she becomes convinced that reconciliation is impossible. Additionally, she may respond to angry outbursts through her attorney, making increasingly unreasonable demands for support, property division and sole custody with limited visitation for the father.

FINANCIAL and MONETARY WORRIES

Economic survival becomes a central worry for both parties during the legal proceedings. For most couples, the cost of dividing a single household into two is substantial. Initially, it may even seem impossible for them to maintain two separate households. This uncertainty can trigger a mix of emotions, including ambivalence, confusion, self-doubt, resentment, and frustration.

Emotions can easily intensify during divorce proceedings, especially when lawyers negotiate back and forth. These negotiations, often driven by the desire to increase billable hours, can lead to exaggerated stances and a feeling of powerlessness. When lawyers get involved, even amicable couples can turn hostile, exacerbating the emotional strain of the process.

THE SILENT MARRIAGE

Silence in a marriage can be a deceivingly subtle yet potent factor that undermines the foundation of the relationship. Initially silence may seem harmless; it may just manifest as an occasional quiet dinner or a lull in the conversation. Prolonged silence, however, can signal deeper issues such as emotional disconnection, unresolved conflicts, and even resentment simmering beneath the surface.

Any lack of communication exacerbates misunderstandings and escalates minor grievances into significant issues. Couples stop openly discussing their needs, desires and concerns and instead make assumptions about each other's thoughts and intentions. These assumptions lead to a breakdown of empathy and compassion, as each partner becomes more focused on defending their perspective rather than understanding their spouse's viewpoint. Without effective communication, conflicts remain unresolved and become insurmountable barriers to the relationship.

Silence in the marriage stifles emotional expression and denies the opportunity to be heard and validated by their partner. Suppressing feelings or avoiding difficult conversations may seem like a solution to maintain peace, but it creates emotional neglect and isolation. Over time, this emotional suppression leads to resentment and bitterness. Their sense of partnership and collaboration erodes, and the couple finds themselves married but leading separate lives. This lack of unity and shared purpose leaves both partners feeling unfulfilled and lonely. Ultimately, silence in the marriage is not just the absence of sound but the absence of connection, understanding and mutual respect. Over time, the cumulative effect of silence and lack of communication create irreparable damage to the bond, leaving couples feeling disconnected and ultimately seeking to separate to find their own voices and reclaim their emotional well-being.

<u>DEAR READER</u>, I'd often watch older couples next to us in restaurants and vow we'd never be like them—those who ate their meals silently. Julia and I promised ourselves that we would always have something to talk about. But as time passed, our promises to each other began to fade. Increasingly, when we watched those older couples in restaurants, we saw our own reflections in their silent exchanges.

It dawned on me that lately, we had only talked about business or work-related matters. Our conversations were devoid of the intimacy and dreams that had once fuelled our relationship.

Whenever I listened to Rupert Holmes's *The Pina Colada Song, Escape*, I envied the carefree spirit embodied in its lyrics, longing for the spontaneity and excitement it promised. Had we become prisoners of routine, trapped in a cycle of work and responsibilities that left little room for spontaneity or romance?

> *I didn't think about my lady*
>
> *I know that sounds kinda mean*
>
> *But me and my old lady*
>
> *Had fallen into the same old dull routine*

There were moments in recent years when I glanced at Julia across the table and realised we had become strangers in our own lives. It's not that I stopped loving Julia. And no matter that a gulf seemed to have crept up between us — I convinced myself that Julia's love for me lingered, and a fragile ember remained. I couldn't help but wonder how we had arrived at this juncture. The truth was our relationship had become a mere shadow of its former self. Julia had become a master of avoidance, tiptoeing around the elephant in the room with practised ease. Neither of us was able to confront the underlying issues that tore us apart, so we continued to drift further apart, weighed down by the burden of unresolved conflicts.

I yearned to live the "Pina Colada Song" Escape; the song lyrics tantalised me with visions of new beginnings and wove fantasies of two people rekindling their flame and finding their way back to each other. Promises of a fresh start—a chance to rewrite our story. If only.

PARENTAL CARE CONCERNS

<u>Divorce is bad enough. It's much worse when there are children.</u>

Child custody, often dubbed as the ugliest of litigation, is characterised by emotional turmoil, accusations, misinterpretations of personalities and life events, and a profound bitterness that exacerbates conflict between you and your ex with detrimental effects on your children. The sheer distortion in perception that a divorce can create makes any issue around them a thousand times worse. It's difficult to remember that the person you now view as a monster was once a loved one and was someone you were once so excited about that you gradually and knowingly built a life together.

The most distressing aspect of custody disputes is the impact on the children. Children may feel trapped amid their parents' conflict; this can result in feelings of anxiety, guilt, and confusion. The influence of lawyers on the parents over child custody during the proceedings is significant. Remember how I said tactics unscrupulous lawyers use can escalate and prolong the divorce process? Lawyers don't care if kids are involved. In fact, children are great points of leverage for generating nice, profitable conflict. Fabrication of information, manipulation of evidence, and exploiting procedural loopholes to undermine the other parent's case are just some of the dirty tactics lawyers use during custody disputes. Stoking feelings of anger, resentment and mistrust toward the other parent, lawyers unnecessarily exacerbate their client's emotions.

One parent may seek to exert control or power over the other by restricting access to the children. In particular, remember that mothers almost always get the benefit of the doubt in the eyes of the legal system during divorce proceedings. The mother may feel a sense of dominance or superiority over the father by withholding visitation rights, especially if there are unresolved issues or conflicts in the relationship.

PSYCHOLOGY OF EGO
EGO IS A DIRTY WORD!

Skyhook's song 'Ego' explores the concept of ego in the context of relationships and self-perception. Ego is often viewed as one's sense of self-importance or self-esteem, and it can significantly impact how people navigate their interactions with others. This is particularly true during a difficult divorce. The psychology of divorce delves into the complexities of ego as individuals grapple with emotions such as loss, rejection, and self-worth. The ego can serve as a shield or as a point of vulnerability, influencing how people perceive their former partners or themselves.

During a divorce process, it is common for the ego to surface as feelings of hurt, resentment, and self-protection come into play. However, allowing it to drive the process can impede negotiations and cause more distress for both parties. Therefore, it is crucial to prioritise clear communication and focus on long-term well-being. This is not just about managing the present, but about securing a healthier future. Recognising that the ego is a delicate aspect of our nature, striving to rise above its influence is essential. By acknowledging ego as a potential obstacle to resolution, everyone can work towards a constructive separation that leads to better outcomes without exacerbating conflicts and unnecessary contention.

Despite the pain and challenges you're now experiencing, it's important to recognise that understanding the psychology of divorce can profoundly impact your journey throughout the divorce and legal processes and then toward healing and renewal. As a Divorced Virgin, you stand at the threshold of a new chapter in your life. It's a chapter filled with growth, transformation, and self-discovery. When you rebuild your life and pursue new goals and aspirations, take comfort in the knowledge that the challenges you face today are shaping you into the resilient, compassionate, and empowered man you are destined to become. Trust in your ability to navigate the divorce process and lean on the wisdom of those who have walked this path before you. Remember that you are not alone. Draw strength from the support of loved ones and seek guidance from trusted mentors and your faith. Better days, far better days, lie ahead for you as a Divorced Virgin.

Honour where you've been while embracing where you're headed.

In the aftermath of divorce, reclaim your identity. The term Divorced Virgin does not connote loss or upheaval; it carries with it a sense of resilience and possibility. We have the power to reinvent ourselves and create a new life that truly reflects our deepest desires.

LOVE STORY
"The person they are."

Julia wasn't the type to embarrass others for amusement. However, when Julia had me escorted to the supermarket's exit door, I could take a little embarrassment, but way back then, my embarrassment was immense.

Although nobody knew it at the time, being a teenager in the 1990s meant you were the last generation to experience a world without ever-present technology. CDs, floppy disks, and dial-up internet were hailed as revolutions in modern living. It was a simpler era, free from the constant pressures of mobile phones and social media— where every move wasn't meticulously tracked. But with that simplicity came the uncertainty of reaching out to someone.

Imagine calling a friend's house and asking their parents if they were available to chat because that house phone was the only means of communication they owned. Consider navigating a conversation with her dad before she even got on the line! The struggle was real. And it's nothing short of a miracle that anyone managed to get through on those phone lines, given that there was exactly one line per house.

On one late summer afternoon, such a miracle happened. Not because it was a case of too many people in my household waiting to use the phone or Julia simply picking up the phone hung between her home's kitchen and family room. Still, it was a miracle that I was lazing in my bedroom one late summer afternoon, and Julia managed to escape her super strict parents' surveillance. Armed with some spare change, she embarked on a covert mission to a payphone several blocks from her home. You know, the kind of phone booth that's like a relic from a bygone era— a place where secrets are whispered and clandestine calls are made.

"Evan...is that you?" she asked timidly.

"Yes it's me, Julia..." I paused, pleasantly surprised.

"You had me thrown out of the supermarket," I continued, for want of something better to say.

"I'm sorry. You never came back, and honestly, I missed the attention," she replied.

Summer romances begin for all kinds of reasons. Summer love is usually the beginning and has always been considered the most romantic of the four seasons. Julia was then in her final year, and I had dropped out and was unemployed, so we had plenty of time to get together. We spent every opportunity to go to the beach, watch movies, and go to lakes and cafes. Julia would either skip classes at school or simply not go at all. Often, I would pick her up from the corner block of her home just so I could spend fifteen minutes with her, taking her to school, then return in the afternoon so I could spend another fifteen minutes taking her back to the corner. We felt we were meant for each other. I never proposed to Julia, not in the sense of down on one knee anyway. We were both far too young, and anyway, it was just a given. We knew we would eventually get married.

Life could not have been better: clear skies, the blazing sun on sandy beaches, gentle summer breezes, and the passion of young love. Of course, eventually, the inevitable happened. We were caught, and Julia's parents were furious. They forbade Julia from ever seeing me again.

"You're about to go to university and make something of your life! He's nothing but an unemployed lout!" they fumed. I was, in fact, unemployed and a first-year university dropout. But I don't think I was a lout. In fact, my situation wasn't very unusual at all.

In the 1990s, Australia faced a severe recession marked by a rapid rise in unemployment. As the Sydney Morning Herald reported, headlines like "10,000 sign up for unemployment benefits in a week" underscored the magnitude of the crisis. The job market struggled to keep pace, with just three available positions for every 100 job seekers. Bankruptcies surged, driven mainly by exorbitant interest rates reaching as high as 17%.

My parents earned a very modest income of three hundred and twenty dollars a week, but I don't recall ever going without. Even with higher interest rates and increased mortgage payments, I was rather spoilt in my upbringing. Dad worked two jobs, and my mother occasionally sewed dresses at home through word of mouth. My mother's (a self-proclaimed sophist) resolve was unyielding—like a boomerang that always comes back, even when you throw it half-heartedly; she walked with me into the unemployment office to return the first cheque that arrived in the mail. She was adamant that I was not to depend on dole payments in the fear that I may get used to solely relying on the benefits to get by.

However, during this downturn, the wedding industry boomed, partially due to the high volume of wedding-related movies released in the

90's—such as *Father of the Bride*, *Four Weddings and Funeral*, and *My Best Friend's Wedding*. In fact, the wedding industry was starting to be considered its own business. This was good news and bad news for brides and grooms of the time - there was far more access to ideas and inspiration for the big day, but this phenomenon also increased the prices of more significant wedding components. Bridal bouquets shrank in size, cakes with fresh flowers began to pop up at receptions all over Melbourne, and brides began to opt for more straightforward floral arrangements.

This was relevant for me because, as noted, my band used to play at weddings. Wedding band fees were determined by their popularity, and I could now earn more in a single weekend than my parents' combined weekly incomes. I would even offer add-ons such as disposable cameras at each table for guests to snap candid photos for additional fun throughout the night — think Monica and Chandler's wedding in Friends!

I refused to stop seeing Julia, even after her father threatened me with a couple of his waiting thuggish friends as I drove into my parent's driveway late one night after playing at a wedding gig.

"Back in my hometown in Caprice, I fled because I stabbed a son of a bitch.", proclaimed one of the thugs.

So, I violently grabbed him with both hands on his shirt collar and repeatedly thrust him on the pale fencing. I honestly didn't know a rusty nail protruding from the picket supporting the pale fencing was stabbing him each time I thrust and pushed him against it. But apparently, it was the rusty nail that made my impromptu defensive reaction a lot more effective.

"Even if you surround her school with your Italian armed forces! I'll fucking dig a tunnel and still get through!" I exclaimed, throwing him onto the concrete pavement before walking away. I felt great for about thirty seconds and then immediately regretted my outburst. I was now certain all hopes of Julia and I being together had ended.

Convinced that Julia would no longer want anything to do with me, the following afternoon, I called the rest of the band members to a practice session in GM Studios to practice our updated repertoires for upcoming wedding gigs. While we were there, improbably enough, I got a call from Julia. She had memorised phone numbers of places where I would most likely be if I weren't home. In the nineties, this was one part of the pain of never being sure you could contact someone.

"HI, Evan! How are you?" she started.

I was about to apologise for the previous night's events when she cut me off.

"I'm so happy; what did you say to my father last night?"

"They love you now!" she exclaimed.

I could not have been more at a loss for words.

"Ahhh, say again?" I asked.

"Tell me what happened….? Tell me what happened with your parents?"

I wondered whether what had happened the previous night had only been a nightmare. Ok… I may have had one or two more than I should have, but didn't I thrash a thug from Caprice? Or did I dream it?

"Apparently, my father's friend thought very highly of you! He convinced my dad that you were genuine. He loved you!" Julia was so excited I didn't know how to respond. "What happened, Evan? Please tell me what you said to him that made my dad change his opinion of you?"

I don't remember exactly what I said to her then, but I do remember that it wasn't the truth. I didn't muster the courage to tell Julia what had really happened the night her father visited me with his thuggish friends until our tenth wedding anniversary.

Being engaged is hyped up to be the most exciting time of your life. After all, you're getting married! She is everything you ever wanted! You're going to live happily ever after! It is a time in the relationship when the expectations are very high for the world and yourselves—as well as the sombre recognition that you are signing up for "better or worse."

Our engagement period can best be described as tumultuous. Traditionally, engagement periods enable couples and their families to become acquainted, except for one problem. My future in-laws didn't share our rosy view of our marriage and did whatever they could to throw a wrench in the spokes. Whatever credit I'd earned with Julia's father by pushing back against his thuggish friends was short-lived and did not extend to the rest of Julia's family. In short, they thought Julia was making a huge mistake.

Our engagement period was full of calamities and close calls with world-ending cataclysms. Julia's mother was constantly critical of my lack of education and couldn't understand why her daughter wanted to marry a taxi driver. Indeed, this is a contradictory standard, considering that neither of Julia's parents had worked for more than seven years since their migration to Australia. They were both swift to learn the benefits of workers' compensation in the mid-eighties.

Naturally, in the face of such opposition Julia and I had a rough go of things. However, we were married after twelve months of countless breakups and immense family wrangles. Sitting in the rear seat of our chauffeured limousine, driving away from the reception, I felt a huge sigh of relief. I had finally married the person of my dreams and my true love. From this point onwards, I felt that there was nothing that I couldn't achieve.

That sense of confidence crumbled after our return flight from our honeymoon to Fiji after realising that the fifty cents of loose change in my pocket was enough to buy…well, nothing. Talk about a reality check! I had to call my parents to pick us up from the airport.

I had to earn some money, especially as Julia was still in school and couldn't work. I wasted no time working fifteen-hour shifts driving conglomerate-owned taxis and doing weekend wedding gigs. Julia continued her university studies, and we lived with my parents in their sizeable double-storey home in Gladstone Park.

I frequently parked at the airport because it allowed me to catch up on sleep while waiting for flights, which tended to be longer fares. As fate had it, one ordinary day, I saw a taxi with a "Taxi for Sale" sign in the rear window parked in front of mine. Excited by the opportunity for a new venture, I approached the driver without hesitation. He was a friendly older man named Allan and explained that he was retiring after many years in the industry.

<u>Dear Reader</u>, blind confidence can propel individuals toward their goals with unwavering determination and belief in their abilities. It's a conviction that success is possible and inevitable, even amid uncertainty and adversity.

However, blind confidence is not without its pitfalls. When not balanced with self-awareness and humility, it can lead people to reckless behaviours, blinding them to their actions' limitations and consequences.

With barely a penny to my name, the deal was done!

But it gets better. Walking back to my taxi, I noticed the driver behind me flipping through a newspaper, pausing now and then to take a sip of coffee.

Desperation and passion are powerful motivators that can propel you forward with an intensity that knows no bounds. Without hesitation, I approached the guy behind me and offered him a 50% share partnership of the taxi that I had just negotiated.

The driver's demeanour shifted.

"I don't even know your name!" he remarked.

"That's okay. I don't know yours either", I replied with a grin.

I was excited to get back home and share the news with Julia before packing up my guitar and equipment for a gig at a restaurant owned by my friend Paul.

I couldn't wait to get home and tell Julia the news.

"Honey... I bought a cab!" I exclaimed

Cue the jaw-dropping silence and the slow blink of disbelief. Her expression was the same as when she had security throw me out of the supermarket.

"With what money?" she asked incredulously.

I expected that response. I played up the benefits of the new venture my fellow cabbie and I had embarked upon together, though I made it a point not to tell her that I had just met the man with whom I was entering into the partnership.

You have to understand the context, though. Australia was still reeling from "the recession we had to have."

Unemployment was still high, and businesses, in general, were struggling to stay afloat. Taxis, however, continued to operate. And now I was in business for myself instead of driving for someone else. The following three years of the partnership were the best I've had. Nothing else ever compared. The arrangement was simple. I would drive the cab throughout the day, and the other guy would drive at night. We kept what we made and split the running costs of the cab.

It worked. Being my own boss meant I kept more of what I made, and having a partner helped share the load enough to be manageable. It was during these three years that Julia and I bought our first home, a quaint but newly- built abode without landscaping, curtains, heating or air conditioning in a new estate nestled on the outskirts of Melbourne's outer northern suburbs, with its quiet streets and the scent of eucalyptus in the air. And soon after moving in, life took another momentous turn with the arrival of our first daughter, Eilleen. Her infectious laughter soon filled every corner of our home, bringing a new-found sense of joy and greater purpose to our lives. We watched as she took her first steps in the backyard and spoke her first word, "Jack !"

Those were great days. I will never forget when we burst into laughter attempting D.I.Y landscaping and installing pop-up sprinklers covered in mud from tip to toe as it rained. Our neighbours Patrick and Rachael on one side and Jim on the other were always there when we needed them—on hot summer evenings, we'd all meet in the court to play cricket or kick a football. Jack, by the way, was the name of Patrick and Rachael's Doberman.

It was the first of many great experiences. Each of these firsts etched unforgettable memories into the fabric of our lives: the first time we experienced the grandeur of a Broadway Show, Sunset Boulevard, the first time we experienced the culinary delights of fine dining at the Melbourne Oyster Bar, the exhilarating acquisition of our family's first brand- new car BMW 320, and our inaugural journey abroad since our honeymoon. These years are eternally inscribed in my soul as a time of profound love and the beginnings of our journey as a family. Something about those memories feels like a warm embrace from the past.

If a time machine existed, I'd leap to revisit those days. I'd give anything to see Julia standing on that front porch, her smile radiant as ever, with little Eilleen cradled in her arms, her tiny hands waving excitedly as my taxi rumbled up the street and into our court. Those moments made every long shift behind the wheel worth it— the moments of pure, unfiltered joy that seemed to suspend time. As I imagine reliving that scene, I can't help but feel a pang of longing for a simpler time in those quiet moments of love and connection that waited for me at home.

Julia often took out our photo albums when our friends or families visited. Ah, that old photo album. It was a relic from a bygone era filled with snapshots of questionable fashion choices and cringe-worthy family portraits, but each photo, lovingly curated and meticulously arranged, reminds us of the stories of our lives. In today's digital age, the photo album has been replaced by the cold embrace of smartphones and cloud storage. Instead of gathering around the coffee table to reminisce over faded photographs, we now scroll through endless streams of pixelated memories, swiping left and right with reckless abandon through thousands of pictures. In contrast, the albums were special. In one of those albums was a picture of me holding Eilleen in my arms just after her birth in the hospital. I must have seen that picture thousands of times and always looked at it fondly, but this time, the blue taxi uniform I wore in the photo seemed to stand out the most to me, clearly showing the taxi company I was affiliated with on my shoulder epaulettes.

I realised one day, looking at the photo, that I was still wearing that uniform! I was still a taxi driver! Sure, I provided well for my family. But I fell into despair when I imagined my worth would not extend far beyond the label society would place upon me and, more importantly, what my daughter's perception of me would be as she grew into her adolescence.

The following morning, around 3:00 a.m., I sprang out of bed, woke Julia, and declared, "That's it!"

"Julia, I will no longer be driving cabs!"

"Argh, please just go back to bed! Can't we talk about it tomorrow?"

The tone of her voice seemed to contain a tinge of desperation and a strong hint of pain. No…, come to think of it, it was more anger.

So wisely, I stopped.

I was never a morning person, and it usually took several cups of coffee and a can of Coke each morning to fully wake up and be alert before my shift in the cab. But this particular morning was different. Dressed in my taxi uniform, I eagerly waited for my partner to bring the cab for the changeover, sitting on my veranda step and smoking my first cigarette of the day. My idea was simple: the partnership agreement with the taxi worked for both of us, but I no longer wanted to drive. By increasing the number of taxis we owned, we could build a small fleet employing drivers and lease a warehouse to maintain and store our cabs. I was sure that my partner would see the potential.

I was shattered, however, when my partner didn't share the same sentiment.

"Evan, you're young and have a young family. But

I'm nearly twice your age and don't have the same passion as you."

The momentum with which I'd started my day very, very early had come to a crashing halt against his immovable refusal.

"The way I see it, you have three choices," he continued.

"Either sell me your share of our cab or;"

"Buy my share out, or we can just sell the cab and go our separate ways. Think carefully throughout the day, Evan, and let me know this afternoon."

Three days passed, and I was still undecided. But Julia highly supported my idea once she was awake enough to hear it.

"Evan, I love you so much. We're always doing new things. If this is what you want and you no longer want to drive cabs, then go for it. Let's buy his share and start looking for our next cab."

Her support for me, her faith in my vision, was crucial at that moment. I'm sure I would not have continued down this road without Julia's support.

Did it work? Well, I stopped driving soon after the fourth cab, and the fleet grew to sixteen taxis within the first two years.

CHAPTER 13
LIQUIDATE THE BUSINESS!

As the echoes of my wife's declaration reverberated through the courtroom, I couldn't help but feel like I was starring in my own twisted episode of "Law and Disorder." Bless his solemn heart, Judge Reinhold looked like he'd just been hit with a legal slapstick routine. Meanwhile, my wife sat there with a smirk rivalling the Mona Lisa's, as if she'd just pulled off the greatest prank in legal history. As for me? Well, I felt like the hapless protagonist in a sitcom gone awry, desperately trying to find the punchline in a situation that was anything but funny. This was now our 17th court appearance in the Federal Circuit Court. Every twist and turn was more baffling than the last, plunging us ever deeper into the abyss of absurdity; I couldn't help but wonder if our saga would end up winning an award for the most absurd courtroom drama. Perhaps we'd even get our own spin-off series: "The Real Housewives of Family Court," I could already envision the tagline, *"In the world of family law, justice is just another word for fucking you over!"*

After a moment of silence that stretched into eternity, Judge Reinhold finally broke the tension with a sigh that sounded more like a defeated groan. "Well," he began, his voice tinged with a mix of resignation and disbelief, "I must say, this was not totally unexpected." Judge Reinhold glanced between Julia and me, "I've seen my fair share of contentious divorce proceedings," he continued dryly. "Still, I must admit, I am curious and concerned about how this matter will pan out."

He paused momentarily, and we waited for the hammer to drop.

"The Federal Circuit Court doesn't have jurisdiction under the Corporations Law to determine the wife's application to appoint an administrator or receiver. Therefore, I have no recourse but to transfer these proceedings to the Family Court of Australia in Melbourne.

<u>Dear Reader,</u> this was a moment that made me want to throw my hands in the air and shout, "Are you fucking kidding me!"

I mean, seriously, why couldn't the legal gods cut me a break for once? Was it too much to ask for a smooth divorce process without all this bull shit?

Apparently so! I felt like storming up to the judge and demanding answers, but then I figured it might not go over too well.

Instead, I settled for some vigorous eyebrow twitching and muttered curses under my breath. Classy, I know. But what would you have done?

We had finally set a date for the trial, and now the whole process was starting over!

Did Julia fully comprehend what she had just done!? Her smile suggested not.

So here we were, back at square one, gearing up for round two of the matrimonial melee.

If laughter is truly the best medicine, then I figured I was in for a heck of a comedic cure.

Thrown out of the Federal Circuit Court and into the Family Court of Australia with a whole new strategy. Julia didn't seem to know when to quit. After failing 17 applications to be reinstated as the company director, amongst other idiotic proposals and forty court-filed applications and documentation, she finally realised the unlikelihood of achieving this goal. So instead she up and decides she'd rather liquidate the business entirely, even though she wasn't entitled to a single penny of it.

Can you hear the episode promo? "In this episode of "Divorce Court Fuck Ups", Julia applies to liquidate the company in the Supreme Court armed with yet another new lawyer in tow!"

<u>Dear Reader</u>, court-ordered liquidation arises when a judge mandates the appointment of a liquidator to dissolve a company. A court-appointed administrator assumes control over the company's day-to-day operations

and business decision-making. This comes at a colossal cost that can only be paid with the assets of the matrimonial asset pool once the divorce process is finalised.

Julia's antics were becoming more audacious with each passing chapter. Despite the mountain of evidence suggesting otherwise, she clung to the belief that liquidating the business would somehow tilt the scales of justice in her favour. Amidst the chaos, drama, and confusion, one thing was certain: court-ordered liquidation is a serious matter with far-reaching consequences. Julia's determination to see the business go up in flames brought us to the Supreme Court just before Christmas.

As for Julia's new lawyer?...

Ah, behold the fledgling legal eagle, fresh out of the academic nest. A wide-eyed novice armed with a briefcase brimming with textbooks and idealism, he marched bravely into the courtroom like a knight in polyester-blend armour. Meet the legal rookie, whose legal acumen is matched only by his fervent belief in the power of Netflix courtroom dramas.

"Good morning, Mr Cutler; my name is Sam Greenhorn," he politely introduced himself, with a handshake firmer than his grasp on legal precedents.

"I represent your ex-wife, Julia."

Despite his rookie status, Sam Greenhorn had a certain charm and earnest enthusiasm. His optimism was infectious, his determination unwavering, and his legal arguments...well, let's say they were a work in progress.

FAMILY LAW ACT 1975

IN THE FEDERAL CIRCUIT COURT OF AUSTRALIA	FILE NO: (P)MLC9445/2014
BETWEEN:	JULIA CUTLER (Applicant)
AND:	EVAN CUTLER (Respondent)
BEFORE:	JUDGE REINHOLD
DATE:	17 December 2015
MADE AT:	MELBOURNE

THE COURT ORDERS THAT:

1. Pursuant to Section 39 of the *Federal Circuit Act 1999*, these proceedings be transferred to the Family Court of Australia at Melbourne, to be listed with such priority as that Court is able to provide.

By the Court

JUDGE REINHOLD

AND THE COURT NOTES THAT:

a. Application for a receiver in made for the Business and that the FCC doesn't have jurisdiction under the Corporations law.

I could see right away that Sam Greenhorn, the rookie lawyer, was clearly out of his league, and I was going to make sure he knew it. It was clear Greenhorn had no solid legal ground to support his claims. But that didn't stop him from trying.

With shaky confidence, Greenhorn began to outline Julia's arguments in a way that seemed more like wishful thinking than legal strategy. His primary argument centred on the notion of fairness and equity. He contended that Julia had a rightful claim to the business assets as we were in divorce proceedings and that liquidating the company was the most equitable solution.

Drawing inspiration from legal precedents and hypothetical scenarios from his extensive Netflix binge-watching sessions, Sam Greenhorn painted a picture of Julia as the victim of circumstance, unjustly deprived of her rightful share of our assets. He leaned heavily on emotional appeals, portraying her as a downtrodden protagonist, a single mother in the tumultuous saga of our divorce proceedings. With a flair for the dramatic and a talent for tugging at heartstrings, he did his best to elicit sympathy from the court.

However, despite his best efforts to portray Julia's actions as justified, the judge's sceptical gaze told a different story, revealing a lack of confidence in Greenhorn's arguments and casting doubt on the validity of Julia's claims. Greenhorn's reliance on emotional appeals and speculative accusations failed to sway the judge, who remained unmoved by his rhetoric.

In the end, the Judge ruled in my favour, stating that there was no legal basis for liquidating my business.

From humble beginnings driving cabs, the business had grown to a fleet of eighty taxis and a sizable limousine and charter bus company. The company was the most extensive transportation provider for the airline industry out of Melbourne Airport, and there was no way I was allowing someone with the legal acumen of a goldfish, flashing a toothy grin that screams, "I watched a season of 'Suits' once, so I'm basically Harvey Specter" undo what I had laboured so long to build.

They say that *hell hath no fury like a woman scorned*, but they haven't met a man determined to protect his business empire. I was a modern-day David against the Goliath of divorce court fuck ups; there could only be one Virgin, my slingshot was full of rocks – and that Virgin was me!

CHAPTER 14
DEPRESSION

Men are more than twice as likely to suffer from post-divorce depression than women.

So now that I've told you about how the courts, in general, and my ex-wife, in particular, conspired to make my life a living hell for years, let's talk about depression a bit.

At its core, depression is more than just feeling sad or blue; it's a pervasive mental illness that impacts every facet of daily existence. You may suffer from distorted perception, disturbed sleep, and changes in appetite. Depression feeds on insecurities and amplifies self-doubt, weaving a tangled web of negativity into a cycle of hopelessness and despair.

In this chapter, we delve into the complex relationship between depression and divorce, exploring how they intertwine.

The end of a marriage can trigger a cascade of emotions ranging from anger and sadness to guilt and shame, all of which can exacerbate existing feelings of depression or give rise to new ones. The loss of a partner, coupled with the dismantling of shared dreams and future plans, can leave you grappling with a profound sense of loss and disconnection. For many, the experience of divorce can also catalyse confronting underlying issues of depression that may have been lurking beneath the surface for years. The upheaval of divorce often strips away the façade of normalcy, forcing the confrontation of the raw, unvarnished truths of our innermost struggles. Anyone entangled in a divorce may find themselves grappling with long-buried emotions, unresolved traumas and deeply engrained patterns of thought and behaviour that contribute to their depression.

The experience of depression during divorce can vary greatly between men and women, influenced by a myriad of factors, including social expectations, cultural norms, and coping mechanisms. While there is no one-size-fits-all approach to navigating the challenges of divorce and depression, there are some common themes and patterns that seem to emerge.

For many women, the process of divorce is deeply intertwined with feelings of grief, loss and betrayal. The end of a marriage can represent the shattering of lifelong dreams and aspirations, leaving women grappling with a profound sense of disillusionment and despair. In addition to the emotional toll of divorce, women may also face practical challenges such as financial security, housing instability, and concerns about their children's well-being. These stresses can exacerbate feelings of depression, leaving women feeling overwhelmed in the face of adversity.

Moreover, women often face distinct societal pressures and expectations during a divorce. Cultural norms around gender roles often dictate that women should prioritise their family's needs above their own, which can lead to feelings of guilt or inadequacy if they are unable to meet these expectations. Additionally, women may be stigmatised by their communities for choosing divorce, adding further stress to an already difficult situation.

Of course, that's not the case for all women. There exists another scenario in which the ex-wife, fuelled by bitterness and a desire for revenge, sets out to push her former husband into the depths of depression for her benefit.

It begins innocuously enough, with subtle jabs and passive-aggressive comments disguised as concern or care. The ex-wife, sensing her former husband's vulnerability, exploits his insecurities and weaknesses, planting seeds of doubt and self-loathing that take in his psyche.

As the divorce proceedings drag on, the ex-wife ramps up her campaign of psychological warfare, using everything and anyone at her disposal to undermine her former husband's mental health. She weaponises the legal system, filing frivolous motions and restraining orders, dragging out court proceedings in a calculated effort to drain his financial resources and erode his resolve. She manipulates their children, using them as pawns in her twisted game of emotional chess, turning them against their father and further isolating him from his support network.

Meanwhile, the ex-wife plays the role of the victim with precision, casting herself as a long-suffering martyr, enduring her ex-husband's alleged abuse and neglect. She becomes the innocent victim of his cruelty, weaving half-truths designed to elicit sympathy from those around her. She revels in her new personal identity (that third person you married- the person they become in family court) and the newfound power that comes with it, relishing the pain and suffering she has inflicted upon her former husband.

In the face of such manipulative and destructive behaviour, it's crucial to prioritise your mental well-being above all else; firstly, believe in staying a Divorce Virgin. Don't get screwed just because you can't give a fuck! We, as men, experience divorce and depression in different ways, influenced by societal expectations around masculinity and emotional expression. We are often socialised to suppress our emotions and to prioritise stoicism and self-reliance, which makes it difficult for us to acknowledge or seek help for our mental health struggles. As a result, we may be more likely to internalise our feelings of depression, leading to superficial impressions of stability but internal feelings of isolation and alienation from our support networks.

Men also face unique challenges during divorce-related issues, such as custody and visitation rights. The fear of losing access to our children or being labelled as unfit parents weighs heavily on our mental health, exacerbating our depression.

What can you do? It's essential to seek support from trusted friends and family members; the right therapist can provide the support and guidance you need.

You can also start dating to counteract the adverse effects of depression.

Dating after divorce can be a complex and multifaceted experience, but for many men, it can act as a powerful remedy for depression. While initially daunting, embarking on a new romantic journey offers renewed hope for the future. It allows for forming new connections and provides much-needed emotional support and validation. That's what I was finding at the café at the courthouse with this private eye straight out of a Bond movie.

As I began my romantic journey with Zoe, the support of friends like Paul proved invaluable. When he texted to ask about my date, I responded with a light-hearted quip: "The date went well! She laughed at my jokes. Either she's into me, or she's compiling a list of intervention orders."

This offbeat, quirky response held a more profound truth. It represented a newfound sense of possibility in overcoming negative emotions. Dating Zoe brought a sense of companionship and validation that I had sorely missed. It was a far cry from the loneliness and isolation I had felt after separating from Julia. Despite my doubts and vulnerability, I embraced the moment and its potential. A new romantic journey may seem daunting at first, but it's a path to renewed hope for the future, forming new connections and providing much-needed emotional support and validation.

And, of course , besides friends and dating, exercises offer a valuable outlet for stress relief. Physical activity allows one to channel pent-up emotions and frustrations into productive movement, releasing tension. For in the act of exercise, there lies a hidden intimacy, sweat, and strain, a byproduct of hard rhythmic exertion of pleasure and ecstasy. It's just not exertion- it's the kind of pleasure that lingers, leaving your muscles tingling with the afterglow of satisfaction.

<u>Dear Reader</u>, if your brain just shifted gear into a double entendre, interpreting double meaning into the last paragraph…for fucks sake, go for a walk and start dating!

CHAPTER 15
THE APPEAL

The Farce of Justice: Appealing Smallcocks' Absurd Final Orders

The Judgement is in…

In the annals of legal history, the colossal clusterfuck of idiocy known as Judge Smallcock is the epitome of a rare breed of incompetence and tomfoolery. His final orders, reeking with contemptuousness and ineptitude, stand as a damning testament to the depths of his intellectual drollery.

In short, he fucked up big time.

Judge Smallcock's final orders left me questioning my possible transgressions in a previous life. His incompetence had turned what should have been a straightforward legal matter into an epic farce.

As I sat in the courtroom, witnessing each of Judge Smallcock's non-sensical decrees and absurd rulings unfold, I couldn't help but marvel at the sheer audacity of his ineptitude. It was breathtaking. But I was now a veteran of the court process. After forty-two court appearances and countless hours of legal wrangling, the decision to appeal and challenge the legitimacy of Smallcock's final orders was already set before Smallcock even finished delivering his judicial buffoonery.

Dear Reader, does this sound familiar? We've come full circle to that farce of a courtroom scene from Chapter 1! But now you've witnessed firsthand my evolution from a lamb teetering on the brink of being ensnared during my initial self-represented appearance in court to the resilient, proud and unwavering Divorced Virgin I have steadfastly become.

In Australia, appeals in family law cases are relatively rare. This can be attributed to several factors. Firstly, family law judgements are discretionary, meaning the judges possess considerable flexibility in their decision-making. This discretionary power makes it challenging to demonstrate that a decision was rendered erroneously. However, about half of the family law appeals pursued in Australia were successful despite this obstacle. And most of the appeals filed were predominately by men!

The need for a more equitable representation of appeals lodged by men within the family law system is becoming increasingly recognised within men's circles. While societal perceptions often cast men as the aggressors or primary providers in family disputes, the reality is far more complex. Men frequently encounter systemic biases and stereotypes that can lead to unjust outcomes in family law proceedings despite the progress made in strides towards gender equality. Men are often disadvantaged by prevailing attitudes and assumptions that favour women. The disparity in how family law cases are adjudicated has profound consequences for men and their families. Unjust rulings impact our financial stability, parental rights, and emotional well-being, exacerbating the already challenging process of separation and divorce.

Despite these challenges, there is a growing recognition that men, too, have the right to fair and impartial treatment within the family law system. By encouraging more men to pursue appeals when unjustly treated, we can work together as Divorced Virgins to rectify systemic injustices and promote equality under the law. I remain steadfast in my journey as a Divorced Virgin, committed to amplifying the voices of men who have been silenced or marginalised within the system.

Divorced Virgin advocates men's rights within the family law system to achieve true gender equality and justice.

In legal proceedings, a Full Court refers to a panel of judges who convene to hear and decide cases, particularly in appellate courts. In many jurisdictions, including Australia, the Full Court comprises senior judiciary members with expertise in the relevant field of law. Three or more judges typically hear appeals from lower courts or tribunals.

During the appeal process, the Full Court considers the arguments presented by the parties and reviews the evidence. It applies the relevant legal principles to determine whether the lower court's decision should be affirmed, modified, or overturned. Their decision is legally binding and represents the final resolution of the appeal within the court system unless a further appeal is permitted to a higher court.

The written Judgment delivered by the Full Court outlines the reasons for the decision and any orders or directions issued by the court.

In the following pages, we'll provide a systematic overview of the legal proceedings that took place in my own case. This will encompass an analysis of the judge's judgement, followed by an examination of my subsequent appeal and the resultant ruling by the Full Court. Throughout this process, I will elucidate each stage's legal grounds, clarifying the rationale behind overturning the judgments.

A successful appeal from the Family Court of Australia to the full court hinges on several critical criteria that must be met to persuade the appellate judges to overturn or modify the original decision. Here's a breakdown of what these criteria typically entail:

Errors of Law

To succeed in an appeal, the appellant must demonstrate that the Family Court's original decision incorrectly applied (or even ignored) applicable law(s) on the books.

Errors of Fact

Appeals may also succeed if the original decision has demonstrable errors of fact. This could involve inaccuracies in the assessment of evidence, failure to consider relevant facts, or findings unsupported by the evidence presented during the trial.

Procedural Fairness

Appellate courts scrutinise whether the proceedings in the Family Court were conducted procedurally fairly. This entails ensuring that both parties were given a fair opportunity to present their case, that relevant evidence was adequately considered, and that the principles of natural justice were upheld throughout the proceedings.

Significant Legal Issues

Appeals may be successful if they raise significant legal issues or points of law that warrant the attention of the Full Court. These could include matters of legal precedent, constitutional importance, or broader societal implications that justify appellate review.

Meritorious Grounds

The success of an appeal often hinges on the strength of the appellant's arguments and legal submissions. Appellants must articulate explicit and compelling grounds for why the decision should be overturned or modified, supported by relevant case law and legal principles.

Judicial Discretion

Appellate courts have discretion in determining whether to intervene in a case. Even if errors of law or fact are identified, the Full Court may choose not to overturn the Family Court's decision if it determines that the outcome was just and equitable based on the circumstances of the case.

Appropriate Relief

This is important: in addition to demonstrating errors in the original decision, appellants must specify the relief sought from the Full Court. This could include varying or setting aside the original orders, issuing new orders, or even remitting the case to the Family Court for further consideration.

Smallcock's monumental blunder was the payment he awarded Julia— totalling a mind-boggling $1,472,000.00 based on only the fleet, amounting to a staggering 60% of the value of the company's rolling stock—including buses and vehicles crucial for day-to-day-operations-. In calculating this payout, he failed to consider the accompanying debts, making this order an error of law.

FAMILY LAW ACT 1975

IN THE FAMILY COURT OF AUSTRALIA

AT MELBOURNE

File No (P) EXXY BGR 2023

BETWEEN

Ms Julia Cutler

Julia CUTLER (Applicant)

AND

Mr Evan Cutler

Evan CUTLER (Respondent)

FINAL PROPERTY ORDER

19 June 2019

PREPARED IN THE REGISTRY

19 June 2019

ORDER 6

On or before 4pm on 20 August 2019 the respondent must pay to the applicant the sum of $1 472 800 being an amount corresponding to 60% of the value of the rolling stock valued by The Valuers.

7. All applications are otherwise dismissed.

I knew this instantly as the cock sucker read out his orders, but that didn't make me feel any better. The wave of emotions standing outside of the courtroom after Smallcock delivered his judgement overwhelmed me. It wasn't just the financial ramifications of Smallcock's screwup that weighed heavily on me or the injustice of my ex-wife capitalising on his error at my expense. The worst part was the cruel sarcasm of seeing her celebrate with her cohorts as they posed for a selfie— yes, a goddamned selfie as if they were just walking out of a Rock Concert or something— using the court foyer as a backdrop for their triumph. As I watched Julia and her sister, Fat Ugly Bertrude, and Scrooge-looking McKenzie friend Mr M Wank, preen and pose for the camera with laughter and smiles, I couldn't help but wonder how they could be so insensitive, so oblivious to the pain they were causing?

As I turned away from the scene, I couldn't hold back the tears any longer. The pent-up emotions burst out, leaving me utterly exposed alone outside the Family Court. I watched Julia and her companions disappear into the distance to where a row of well-established trendy cafés, somewhat ghoulishly, was infamously known to host divorce parties. To me, divorce parties always seem like a paradox— a celebration representing the end of something once cherished. I've struggled to comprehend the rationale of turning a sombre occasion into a festive affair.

The irony of it all was not lost on me—Smallcock's blunder had handed Julia a victory on a silver platter—a total payout order exceeding over 3.5 million dollars, including property orders. Julia believed she had won the lottery, but the victory also exposed cracks in her façade. Now, she fully transitioned into the third person I didn't know I married—the person she had become in the family court. The woman I had loved and trusted was now well and truly gone.

For me, there would be no divorce party—just somebody I used to know.

APPLICATION TO THE FULL COURT

Even dazzled by her triumph, Julia ought to have known I couldn't let this decision stand without appeal.

Dear Reader, *The upcoming pages provide a comprehensive overview of the principles, procedural rules, evidentiary standards, and a summary of arguments related to my appeal, along with reasons for the judgement. Feel free to jump ahead to Chapter 16 and return to this section as needed.*

Successfully navigating the complexities of family law appeals requires a deep understanding of relevant legal principles, procedural rules, and evidentiary standards. A Notice of Appeal must be filed within 28 days from the date of judgment. This timeframe is crucial, as failing to file the notice within the prescribed period may result in losing the right to appeal, barring exceptional circumstances.

The process for appealing a decision from the Family Court of Australia to the Full Court involves several steps:

Filing a Notice of Appeal

This crucial document formally notifies the court of your intention to appeal. It must include a clear outline of the grounds for appeal and the specific orders sought.

Later, you'll see my detailed submission to the Full Court, crafted in response to Smallcock's order. This submission is relevant mostly to my own unique case, of course, but I hope it provides valuable insight into the appeal's procedural aspects and familiarises you with the terminology commonly used throughout the appellate process. By examining my submission closely, you will better understand the procedures involved and become acquainted with the legal language essential for navigating the appeal effectively.

Preparation of Appeal Book

This is a comprehensive compilation of documents, evidence, and transcripts essential for presenting your case to the Full Court. Here is a more detailed elaboration on the preparation of the appeal book:

Identification of Relevant Documents:

The first step in preparing the appeal book is identifying all relevant documents, including court orders, pleadings, affidavits, exhibits, and other materials pertinent to the case. This involves a thorough review of the court record from the original proceedings.

Collation and Organisation:

Once the relevant documents have been identified, they are collated and organised logically and sequentially within the appeal book. Each document should be clearly labelled and indexed for easy reference.

Transcripts of Proceedings:

These transcripts must be purchased from court-authorised providers only. They provide a verbatim record of the oral arguments, witness testimony, and judicial rulings that occurred during the trial or hearing.

Certificate and Pagination

Before finalising the appeal book, it must be certified as a true and accurate record of the documents and transcripts. This certificate is typically provided by a court officer or the appellant's legal representative. Additionally, each page of the appeal book should be numbered sequentially for easy navigation.

Service on the Respondent:

Once the appeal has been prepared and certified, copies must be served on the respondent(your ex-wife) following the relevant procedural rules. This ensures both parties have access to the same materials and can adequately prepare for the appeal hearing.

Submission to the Full Court:

Finally, the completed appeal book is submitted to the Full Court for consideration. It is a comprehensive reference guide for the justices reviewing the case and deciding on the appeal.

Dear Reader: Overall, preparing the appeal book requires meticulous attention to detail and thorough organisation to ensure that all relevant materials are correctly presented to the Full Court. By compiling a comprehensive and well-organized appeal book, appellants can effectively support their arguments and strengthen their case on appeal. Basically, as with all court procedures, it pays to do your homework and do it properly.

Once the appeal is formally filed, documents are prepared, and copies are served to the other side, then the fun begins.

Filing Submissions

You and your ex may then file written submissions with the full court outlining your legal arguments and addressing the grounds of appeal.

Oral Hearing

The Full Court will schedule an oral hearing in which both parties present their arguments before the court's justices. This allows further clarification and examination of the issues raised in the appeal.

Judgement

After considering the written submissions, evidence, and oral arguments, the Full Court deliberates and delivers its judgement. This judgement may uphold, modify, or entirely overturn the original decision of the Family Court.

Enforcement of Judgement

Once the Full Court has rendered its judgement, the parties must comply with its orders. If necessary, enforcement proceedings may be initiated to ensure compliance with the court's decision.

Dear Reader, Smallcock made seven jurisprudential orders. The Full Court dismissed all but one after examining the evidence and deliberations aimed at ensuring a just outcome. The following pages give compelling evidence that they should have reversed all seven.

FAMILY LAW ACT 1975

IN THE FULL-COURT

OF THE FAMILY COURT OF AUSTRALIA

AT MELBOURNE

Appeal No. SOA69 of 2019

File No. MLC.XXYZ of 2014

BETWEEN

EVAN CUTLER
Appellant Husband

and

JULIA CUTLER
Respondent Wife

SUMMARY OF ARGUMENT
For the Appellant Husband

GROUND 1 — error in calculating the value of the existing legal and equitable interests of the parties in the "rolling stock" of the business conducted by the Appellant

1. By paragraph 6 of the Orders made 19 June 2019 the Appellant is required to pay to the Respondent a sum calculated to equal 60% of the value of the "rolling stock" of the business.

2. The Judgment records the conclusion that the "rolling stock" was a separate and unencumbered asset to be divided in the same proportions as the other "assets to be divided".

3. In fact, the "rolling stock" had already been taken into account in the valuation of the business entities, and it was fully encumbered, resulting in a "triple counting" of the "rolling stock".

4. Inclusion as an asset of the business:

    a. Valuation evidence from a single expert and the Appellant's adversarial expert was before the Court.

    b. Both Valuers agreed the valuation of the parties' interests in the businesses should be determined on a net asset basis and at nil negative value. That evidence recorded the business plant and equipment at book values and the corresponding hire purchase liabilities at the time of valuation —

c. The trial judge accepted and adopted the experts' opinions and nil valuation

d. However, the judgment then records that the trial judge introduced, apparently at the wife's urging, the "rolling stock" as a separate item of property. Neither party, in fact, advocated that approach

5. Failure to take account of liabilities associated with the "rolling stock".

   a. The trial judge sought evidence of the value of the "rolling stock" and the finance secured against it.

   b. The parties and the trial judge obtained and adopted a valuation of $2,453,0333.00.

   c. c. The Husband's evidence recorded (albeit not with the precision the trial judge had sought) the various debts encumbering the business vehicles, including $2,913,619 in vehicle finance. The Wife's evidence also referred to Lender Bank and 16 hire purchase leases for business vehicles and annexed a selection of relevant documents.

   d. The Husband complied with the trial judge's directions, providing the Wife with copies of the relevant documents evidencing the liabilities he relied on. The folder of documents was handed to the Court but does not appear on the Exhibit Sheet. The Husband seeks to rely upon that folder of documents.

   e. The Judgment and Order 6 disregard any liability attached to the "rolling stock".

6. The trial judge has, therefore, "double counted" the asset of "rolling stock" by including the valuation of $2,453,033.00 in addition to the nil valuation of the business, which had already taken it into account and, in effect ", triple counted" it by failing to take into account the finance (and other) liabilities attaching to it. The exercise of discretion by the trial judge has, therefore, proceeded upon errors of fact, which give rise to a decision which is plainly wrong 1.

FULL COURT APPEAL GRANTED

FAMILY COURT OF AUSTRALIA

CUTLER & CUTLER AND ANOR   *2019] EXXY 93980322*

FAMILY LAW – APPEAL – APPLICATION IN AN APPEAL – Where the husband sought leave to adduce further evidence – Where the uncontested evidence available at trial is enough to demonstrate appealable error –

ORDERS MADE 27 NOVEMBER 2019

1. The Application in an Appeal filed on 1 October 2019 be dismissed.
2. The appeal be allowed.
3. Orders 2-7 inclusive made on 19 June 2019 be set aside.
4. The parties' applications for property settlement be remitted to the Family Court of Australia for rehearing by a judge other than the primary judge.
5. The Court grants to the appellant-husband a costs certificate pursuant to the provisions of s 9 of the *Federal Proceedings (Costs) Act 1981*, which is a certificate that, in the opinion of the Court, it would be appropriate for the Attorney-General to authorise payment under that Act to the appellant-husband in respect of the costs incurred by the appellant-husband in relation to the appeal.

THE APPEAL

REASONS FOR JUDGEMENT OF THE FULL COURT

Ground 1

1. This ground of appeal contended that the primary judge erred in calculating the value of the parties' existing legal and equitable interests. The error results from the primary judge treating plant and equipment (referred to as "rolling stock") of a corporate business, already accounted for within expert valuations, as a separate and unencumbered asset to be divided between the parties when the rolling stock was indisputably a corporate asset, as valued, to which substantial liabilities attached.

2. The wife did not contend, before the primary judge, that the rolling stock was an asset of the parties, though the primary judge mistakenly recorded she did so. The husband cross-examined the wife, contending the rolling stock was a corporate asset, and the debt encumbering it was a corporate liability, though his evidence-in-chief and his final submissions on the issue were less than entirely clear.

3. Regardless, the expert evidence proceeded upon financial statements and other documents demonstrating that the rolling stock was an asset of one or another of the corporations in which the spouses hold shares, and the primary judge found the asset "formed part of the [husband's] corporate operations". Based on the evidence of two experts, the primary judge found the relevant corporate businesses to have no commercial value, so the value of the rolling stock was already factored into that calculation. Consequently, the rolling stock was double-counted by identifying it at its gross value among the spouses' personal assets. Neither spouse submitted for the rolling stock to be identified as a personal asset, nor did either spouse contend that there were no substantial liabilities relating to the rolling stock.

4. Even if the rolling stock had been a personal asset of the spouses, another error was made by the primary judge in failing to discount its value by the amount of debt encumbering it. At trial, the husband deposed to "vehicle liabilities" of $2,913,619, about which he cross-examined the wife. She admitted that amount was "roughly" the overall quantum of the liability, having earlier been deposed to the current existence of multiple "hire purchase leases" for corporate vehicles, which she allegedly guaranteed. The husband's Application

in an Appeal filed on 1 October 2019 sought leave to address the issue by adducing further evidence in the appeal of the corporate liabilities related to the vehicles, but that application will be dismissed because it is unnecessary to grant leave. The uncontested evidence available at trial, some duplicating the proposed additional evidence, is enough to demonstrate appealable error. As the expert evidence at trial plainly revealed, the primary reason the corporate businesses had no commercial value on either a future maintainable earnings basis or on a net asset backing basis was because of the existence of substantial liabilities.

5. Although not the subject of any ground of appeal, another error was also made as to the precise value of the rolling stock. The primary judge found its gross value was $$2,153,033.00, but the figure of $2,453,033.00 was later transposed to compute the payment due to the wife under Order 6. In isolation, that error could have been rectified under the slip rule.

6. These errors were intrinsic to the findings about the identity and value of the spouses' property interests, which, therefore, vitiate the orders.

I was confident in my case, but that didn't mean it was easy.

CHAPTER 16
SCATTER GUN AT BEST!

Winning the appeal had me grappling with a complex mix of emotions. Relief was mingled with sorrow, gratitude with resentment. I overheard snippets of conversation between Julia and her barrister, acknowledging with certainty that the appeal would be granted even before the Full Court convened. Listening to their conversation, I recalled Smallcock's dismissive remark about my appeal application being "scattergun at best." Clearly, his assessment was just as lousy as his judgment. A sense of vindication washed over me— a quiet satisfaction of the strength of my character and testament to my unwavering determination to protect my "Divorce Virginity".

But amidst the satisfaction of the appeal outcome, as per order four of the appeal court remitting our case to be reheard by a judge other than Smallcock,

4. The parties' applications for property settlement be remitted to the Family Court of Australia for rehearing by a judge other than the primary judge.

...the prospect of facing yet another legal battle, with Smallcock's incompetence still fresh in my mind, wasn't as daunting as I once thought. This is because, in part, when a judge's orders are reversed or set aside, at the very least, his judicial errors or incompetence will damage the judge's reputation amongst his colleagues and legal professionals. Additionally, a judge whose orders are consistently overturned or criticised for incompetence may face professional consequences ranging from reprimand or even removal from the bench. However, disciplining judges is complex and politically sensitive.

I was initially smug, knowing that referring this case to a different judge undoubtedly would serve as a cautionary tale for other judges, reminding them of the importance of the consequences of lapses in judgment or incompetence.

My smugness, however, was relatively short-lived as the COVID-19 pandemic soon upended our lives. It brought about an unexpected and unprecedented change in the world in ways we could never have anticipated. Our lives became suddenly uncertain as lockdowns, travel restrictions, and social distancing became the norm. And worst of all, it slowed everything down – including the court system. Having mastered (or so I thought) the ins and outs of the courts after more than forty court appearances, my experience was thrown out the window as the world rewrote the rules for how everything worked. It took ten months before Justice Shiva was appointed as the new judge, and by then, videoconferencing with Zoom had become the new way of conducting court appearances.

But whether in person or via a computer monitor, I was still determined to get justice.

CHAPTER 17
LOVE STORY

SOMEBODY THAT I USED TO KNOW

"The person they become in ~~(Family Court)~~"
                the UNDERWORLD

A s I sat alone in my dimly lit study, glazing at the ocean beyond my window, I strummed the melancholy melody of a familiar song, "Somebody That I Used to Know" by Gotye, which seemed to echo the sentiments of my being. With a half bottle of Johnny Blue, a slowly burning cigarette perched on the edge of a full ashtray, I had a weathered and worn guitar on my lap – an old instrument that carried the weight of years, the varnish worn thin and frets worn smooth from countless hours of playing. As my pick roamed across the strings, I was filled with a sense of nostalgia and longing:

> *But you didn't have to cut me off*
> *Make out like it never happened that we were nothing*
> *And I don't even need your love*
> *But you treat me like a stranger, and that feels so rough,*
> *No, you didn't have to stoop so low*
> *Have your friends collect your records and then change your number*
> *I guess that I don't need that, though*
> *Now you're just somebody that I used to know*

When divorce enters the picture, you see your partner through a kaleidoscope, revealing previously unseen facets of them. The person you thought you knew so intimately becomes a stranger; the third bride unveiled isn't the blushing young maiden who said "I do" and pledged eternal love. It's the one you never anticipated, the alter ego, the courtroom baroness with a newfound sense of entitlement. That's the version of Julia I met in this absurdly protracted legal drama. And yet, despite the bitterness, my love for her remained. It wasn't a sentiment rooted in any desire for reconciliation— that ship had already sailed — but rather a recognition of the significance of our shared 23-year history as a family.

Our connection was permanently cut off once Julia had the IVO issued and then acted to have me arrested repeatedly for alleged breaches of the same. For years, Julia had me convinced that I was the poster child for narcissism—playing armchair psychologist, drilling into me that narcissistic personality disorder personified. She had me twisted in knots, at least partly believing what she said. Because let's face it: who knows you better than your wife?

Dear Reader, let's dissect Julia's allegations, shall we?

First up, the preoccupation with fantasies of unlimited success-. Guilty as Charged! Who doesn't fantasise about ruling the world from a golden throne? But apparently, dreaming big equals narcissism!

Next, she accused me of having a grandiose sense of self-importance and entitlement. Sure, I believe in working hard and the importance of delegating work to my team, but that doesn't translate to me thinking I'm the King of Dicks, demanding the best seats every time I call Ticketek!

Last but not least is the need for excessive love, admiration, or boasting. Please spare me the theatrics! Sure, I like to talk up my accomplishments; who doesn't? But apparently, in her eyes, that makes me the Sultan of Show-offs.

I'm the narcissist extraordinaire!

It wasn't until I was invited to attend a self-healing retreat that the penny dropped on the truth behind Julia's "diagnosis". The retreat was pretty standard- you know the drill: stand up, introduce yourself, and confess your sins. "Hi, I'm Evan, and I'm a Narcissist", I muttered to the group.

Kellie, a psychologist who was one of the retreat organisers, looked curious. "Evan, why don't you tell us a little bit about those heated arguments with Julia?"

And so, with a heavy heart and a sense of déjà vu, I spilled the beans about my personal failings, as detailed by Julia, culminating in her firm conviction that I was a narcissist.

"Julia would ice me out for what felt like an eternity," I confessed, my voice tinged with frustration and resignation. "I'd apologise endlessly, even when I knew I wasn't entirely to blame, but it was like talking to a brick wall."

Kellie put a reassuring hand on my shoulder.

"Evan, a narcissist, never apologises, and I've yet to meet one that openly admits to having narcissistic characteristics," Kellie said in a soothing tone.

Narcissists don't do apologies!? Seriously?

In fact, after our separation and throughout the torment of the trial, it became glaringly apparent that Julia's lack of empathy or emotional awareness was much more narcissistic than anything she had been accusing me of for years. I realised that Julia's accusations were merely reflections of her own shortcomings.

One can never truly fathom the depths that lie behind a seemingly ordinary expression. That lesson struck me hard when I realised nothing could have prepared me for this; I never thought Julia was capable of being this "third person". The divorce proceedings revealed a side of Julia I hadn't fathomed- But this went far beyond the courtroom drama, beyond the solicitors, barristers and even the incompetent judges. The divorce proceedings had turned merciless. Julia, the woman who wept watching Ghost and Father of the Bride and cared for our children, had orchestrated a diabolical scheme worthy of any crime thriller.

Beneath the skin of familiarity, the truth often lies buried and unspoken.

To understand just how dark things got, I need to give you some background about the city where we lived. **Melbourne**, a city known for its vibrant arts scene and picturesque laneways, harbours a darker side. The 1990s and early 2000s marked a tumultuous period in Melbourne's history, an era known infamously as the Gangland Wars. Underworld figures like

Carl Williams, Tony Mokbel, and the Moran family dominated headlines and cast a long shadow over Melbourne streets. Melbourne witnessed 36 retributive killings involving underworld figures during this period. But the criminal activities extended beyond drug dealings. These underworld figures also operated lucrative rackets in King Street nightclubs, facilitated prostitution rings, and ran illegal gambling operations.

Some took on the role of "negotiators", arbitrating unresolvable disputes with a heavy hand. Interestingly, I grew up in Broadmeadows, and I remember Carl Williams from the neighbourhood. Later, as an adult, I lived in Moonee Ponds, which was not far from the Morans.

I know this partly because of a friend with connections to this sordid side of the city. Tarik Solak. He immigrated to Australia from Turkey in 1969. He started training as a martial artist; his combination of physical skills and showbiz acumen guided him to help kickboxing surge in popularity. He became hugely successful in the early 2000s, capturing audiences worldwide and elevating the sport to new heights of mainstream appeal. Along the way, he also forged friendships with some of Melbourne's most notorious underworld figures.

My friendship with Tarik Solak predated his accent to kickboxing celebrity status. As I immersed myself further into the realm of event and concert promotion across Australia and Spain, our bond deepened. One day, during the endless tedium of my divorce proceedings, he called me up.

"Evan, come around later tonight. We'll shoot some pool, and I have something I need to tell you."

When I arrived at his place, he wasted no time getting to the point

"Some people are asking a lot of questions about you," he revealed. "people you don't want to meet. Just found out Julia is behind it."

Initially, I brushed off his warning. Tarik liked to stir shit up, and I thought he was trying to get a rise out of me. Also, I couldn't entertain the notion that what he was saying could be true. I ran a clean business and had no idea why anyone would be interested in messing with me. Even Julia, I figured, wouldn't stoop this low. Would she?

But Tarik initiated a call with Julia's underworld acquaintance, who then added Julia to the call without telling her. And to my absolute shock, I heard Julia, unaware that both Tarik and I were listening in on speakerphone, talk with a guy about her plot "to do whatever is necessary" to coerce me into settling the divorce on her terms.

She made out like we never happened and that we were nothing.

It was a bitter pill to swallow. The gravity of Julia's betrayal couldn't sink in; I felt a profound sense of disbelief over her callous disregard for our shared history.

What happened to the pretty checkout girl I used to sneak around with? What happened to the enthusiastic and supportive spouse who had encouraged me to grow the business from an idea and half a cab into a multi-million-dollar outfit?

What the actual fuck had happened?

I was somebody she used to know, but I am also somebody she would never forget.

After that call, I was in shock. But Tarik kept up his usually jovial demeanour after the phone call, breaking the silence with a reassuring tone, "Mate, I know it's a lot to take in; don't worry about it. No one's going to stand over you."

Fate is a curious concept that a predetermined path guides our lives in both seen and unseen ways. For me, fate is basically what we make of it. Ironically, Julia's underworld acquaintance unexpectedly crossed paths with me again, but in a different context this time. A well-known cosmetic brand he had recently acquired became a sponsor for a major concert gig and several events I had organised. Indeed, it is a strange twist of fate.

I don't know how far Julia would have taken it, but I do know that Tarik's insight and support were an important and valuable wake-up call on this journey. Sadly, sometime later, he succumbed to cancer after a courageous battle. His fight, one that even this capable fighter couldn't win, was a testament to the true meaning of resilience. He embraced his passing with acceptance and peace... So, I'd like to say thank you, Tarik, for your friendship and your truths. My journey through this divorce process has been hell (see all the other pages of this book,) but your support made it a little more bearable.

CHAPTER 18
COVID

You've read plenty about how my life was turned upside down. Now let's get to a bit where everyone else's life was screwed up as well.

The Great Toilet Paper Fiasco of 2020 will go down in history as one of the most bizarre episodes of human behaviour in times of crisis. Aussies stocked up on toilet paper with an almost religious fervour. Many embraced the "iso-beard" as a symbol of their found freedom rather than lack thereof; with ridiculous lockdown measures in place and hairdressers forcibly closed, Aussies across the country let their hair and beards run wild, with varying degrees of styles from bushy lumberjack beards to scraggy quarantine staches. It was quite a site to see, except, of course, nobody got to see anybody else unless they were wearing a mask – a mask more than likely overstuffed with an excess of facial hair.

The COVID-19 pandemic not only disrupted daily life but also relationships. As lockdown measures were implemented worldwide, couples spent unprecedented time together, leading to moderately heightened tensions.

Before the onset of the pandemic, divorce rates were already a topic of concern in many countries, with factors such as infidelity, financial issues, and communication issues contributing to marital discord. However, the arrival of COVID-19 and subsequent lockdowns confined couples to their homes for extended periods, with limited opportunities for socialising, recreation or escape from the repetitiveness of daily life. For some couples, the increased time spent together during lockdowns provided an opportunity for deeper connection and intimacy. They had more time to communicate and engage in shared activities and rediscovered the importance of companionship.

However, for others, the strain of the lockdown exacerbated pre-existing issues within the relationship. The aftermath of COVID-19 lockdowns saw a significant uptick in divorce filings across the globe. The family courts reported surges in divorce inquiries and court filings as couples sought to dissolve their marriages and move forward with their lives.

And let's not forget the flight bans, because nothing said, "Let's contain the virus," better than forcing airlines to ground fleets, cancel flights, and implement cost-cutting measures because the virus travelled the world faster than DC's Justice League.

Those flight bans were particularly hard for me because my business came to a grinding halt with the grounding of flights. The very business Julia attempted to seize and later sought to liquidate found itself crippled by a microscopic adversary. Australia's lockdown policies, particularly Andrews Government Victoria, ranked among the most stringent globally.

That was the straw that broke the camel's back for me. Lengthened enforced stay-at-home orders, restricted non-essential travel, the closing of businesses and public spaces, and (let's not forget!) a shortage of toilet paper was enough for me to decide to get the fuck out! Australia didn't hold much for me at the time other than the promise of endless court dates. Julia had proven more destructive than I could have imagined; I couldn't see my children thanks to the falsely filed IVO's and I was continually being arrested for their alleged breaches. Even my brief romance with Zoe, which had injected a much-needed dose of confidence and light into my life, appeared to be going nowhere. It was time to escape.

OK! IT'S MID-LIFE CRISIS TIME

With "property issues to attend to" in Spain, I qualified for essential travel prerequisites, prompting me to book the next **First Class** (the *first sign of mid-life, adopting the "Fuck it" attitude*) Qatar flight to Madrid. Upon arrival, I saw that Spain's restrictions were considerably more relaxed, particularly as the country approached the summer months. While vaccination efforts gained momentum globally and Australia persisted with its stringent lockdown protocols, Spain gradually began easing restrictions and re-opening its economy. With Spain's more relaxed stance towards restrictions, there was a sense of optimism as businesses bustled with activity and people reclaimed a semblance of normalcy, a stark contrast to the sombre atmosphere I had left behind in Australia.

Spain's greatest asset has always been its people. From the rhythmic beats of flamenco echoing through cobblestone streets to the joyous chaos of La Tomatina before COVID-19, Spanish traditions are a vibrant reflection of its people's spirit. Being here, far away from the troubles of my homeland, was a balm to my fractured self.

I was sitting in a sidewalk café, slowly sipping an espresso, when I was drawn to a juxtaposition of old and new— a weathered "post no bills" sign standing next to a freshly erected billboard bearing the words, "Live Your Legend."

Several Harley Davidson advertisements have left an impression on me over the years; call it what you will, "a midlife crisis" –a tongue-in-cheek ultimate rite of passage reaching the halfway mark and the timeless tradition of buying a Harley Davidson. Because when you hit that magical age where your hairline starts receding and your waistline starts expanding, nothing says "Fuck it" better than hitting the open road with the roar of a V-twin soft-tail Fatboy Cruiser! So, it didn't take much then to nudge me from that café table to the nearest Harley Davidson dealer.

From the moment I stepped into the dealership, I felt the unmistakable ambience of Harley-culture. Amongst the rows of gleaming motorcycles stood the iconic silhouette of the Fatboy, with its wide front end, solid disk wheels, and signature chrome, all part of its allure.

I wandered through the dealership for hours, my mind drifting over and over again to thoughts of Julia. I imagined what she'd say if we were still together. She would have rolled her eyes at my newfound obsession and, at the very least, iced me for several months.

I don't know if it was the roar of engines and the scent of leather or an act of rebellion against the new COVID world, but maybe we should just call it by what it is—a definite Midlife Crisis. I couldn't help but feel a sense of liberation as I twisted the throttle and rumbled out of the dealership.

There's something about the rumble of a Harley that screams, "I'm not ready for retirement homes and lawn bowling just yet!" I like to think of it as a middle finger to the mundane. Of course, the association between midlife and buying a Harley Davidson has become a bit of a punchline; let's face it, the Harley Davidson is the ultimate Fuck You of midlife rebellion. Let's acknowledge the elephant in the room. So, you hit your forties or fifties, going through a nasty divorce, wondering if this is all there is to life, and then it hits you: "I need a Harley!": Harley Davidson isn't just a motorcycle; it's a lifestyle. And, of course, it comes with the inevitable midlife crisis accessory: the leather jacket. Nothing says "I'm having a meltdown," like dressing like a reject from a 90's rock band.

But hey, who said midlife had to be boring? Sure, you could buy a sports car or take up extreme sports. Still, there's something undeniably exhilarating about a two-wheeled death machine hitting the open road and leaving everything behind in the rearview mirror.

Despite the inevitable raised eyebrows and concerned looks from friends and family, embracing your *Easy Rider* inner badass when life hands you a midlife crisis is a definite statement that you're not going quietly.

My unplanned Harley adventure felt akin to gearing up for the most thrilling bull-run imaginable. Departing from the bustling tapas bars of Madrid's Plaza Mayor, I headed south towards Andalusia. Along the way, I journeyed down the winding roads that meandered through Toledo and Cordoba and the labyrinthine alleyways of Seville's old town.

Throughout the COVID-19 pandemic, Jasmine, my friend here, had remained with her mother in Grenada. Back when Julia's brother unexpectedly confronted me in his apartment, it dawned on me that I had never expressed my gratitude to Jasmine for covering my hospital expenses. I felt a strong desire to visit her, so I reached out via WhatsApp and set out for the ride without even waiting for a response back. I knew I could do a 300 km ride from Seville to Grenada in about 3.5 hours to have dinner with Jasmine, and if she didn't respond, I would just check into my hotel for the night and meet with her the following day.

However, a surge in COVID-19 cases caught me off guard, resulting in localised lockdowns in regions like Grenada. When Jasmine kindly offered their spare room for me to stay, I found myself torn. Of course, I preferred not to be confined to a hotel room, but staying with Jasmine and her mother, while familiar, still felt somewhat awkward. But she did her best to make me feel welcome.

"Looks like you're stuck with me Evan, but I'm so glad you made it," she exclaimed brightly.

"My Mum has been literally driving me mad, and HEYYY, NICE BIKE !" she added excitedly, wrapping me in a welcoming hug.

I wasn't complaining about the welcome. Mid-life crisis, remember?

"Come on, come in, let's get you settled. Mum and I prepared your favourite tapas," she said, grabbing one of my saddle bags with one hand while pulling me towards her garden gate with the other, just as I unstrapped the saddlebag on the other side.

As we stepped inside, the tantalising aroma of Spanish cuisine filled the air. On a rustic wooden table in the rear terrace garden, glistening slices of bresaola and duck prosciutto, the finest Spanish cured meats, nestled beside plump green and black olives marinated in garlic-infused olive oil. But the piece de resistance was the platter of paella, adorned with plump mussels, shrimp, and smoke-infused squid.

Around the table, laughter and conversation flowed freely. Whether the white wine Jasmine was sipping on or the Cabernet Sauvignon I loved influenced our mood, there was a sense of togetherness as the last traces of daylight faded into dusk. I was so grateful for Jasmine and her mother; I felt at home, a feeling that I had missed much more than I had realised.

As the evening drew to a close, our lively chatter subsided, and Jasmine's mum bid us a peaceful good night before heading off to rest. This left Jasmine and me to enjoy the tranquillity and the last few drops of our wines.

"Evan, since the COVID lockdown, she's made me crazy with her conspiracy theories, rearranging furniture for the umpteenth time, and a newfound passion for being a gourmet chef," she whispered, almost uncontrollably laughing.

Her laughter was light, carefree, and utterly infectious. I couldn't help but smile and laugh along with her, forgoing any worries and stresses I had unwittingly packed with me to Spain. But best of all, as we continued to share stories into the night, Jasmine did not once broach the subject of my divorce, instead choosing to focus on precisely what I needed: *ESCAPE*.

Over the next two days of lockdown, Jasmine and I continued to make the most of our time together. Jasmine's dining table became the focal point of the living area. After breakfast, the table became a dedicated workspace for an ambitious project—assembling a 3696-piece Lego Lamborghini Sian. Throughout the day, we took leisurely walks through the winding streets of Granada, but it was the evenings when we were in Jasmine's cosy home over dinner that I savoured the most.

Her mother's cooking was an ongoing revelation, and with the three of us in the kitchen, an unexpected sense of reluctance grew within me—reluctance for the inevitable end of our time together and a pang of sadness at the thought of leaving it all behind. Ironically, amid the lockdown, I found a sense of belonging here.

On the last day of lockdown, the narrow streets of the ancient city lined with centuries-old buildings showed some signs of activity once more as shopkeepers prepared their storefronts while café owners set out tables and chairs on the cobblestone sidewalks, ready to welcome patrons seeking respite, not only from the summer heat but having been in isolation throughout the weekend. Staring up at the Sierra Nevada mountains, I was tense at the thought of riding back to Madrid but was also in awe of the clouds gathering overhead and the distant rumble of thunder, a gentle caution of an impending storm. It made me think a bit of the legal drama still waiting for me back home.

As the first raindrops fell, people emerged from their homes, faces turned upwards, arms in the air as if to greet the cool touch of water on their skin. Jasmine ran ahead. Her laughter mingled with the patter of raindrops, twirling and spinning with grace and abandon. Her wet hair cascading around her shoulders in blonde curls framed her face, and her wide-open mouth and tongue stretched out radiated with infectious joy.

"C'mon Evan, dance with me"! she urged, extending a hand in invitation. "Don't be such a dork", she insisted, her enthusiasm contagious.

"C'mon!!" her persistence was undeniable.

I was drawn to Jasmine in a way I couldn't explain. (Well, okay, I could, but I had been studiously avoiding thinking about it.) With trembling hands, I reached out to touch her, and then, in a moment that defied rationality, I kissed her.

Well, the heavens did open up, not because of the kiss, but unleashed a torrential downpour as the rainwater rushed towards the nearest drains, flooding the streets like little rivers.

"Well, you certainly made this awkward," she quipped, a mischievous glint in her eye as we stood, both drenched by the downpour.

"Jasmine, come with me to Cabo de Gata tomorrow and let's just see where to from there."

With a playful roll of her eyes, followed by a pregnant pause, she said, "Alright, Evan. Cabo de Gata it is. But you tell my mother," her voice brimmed with anticipation, playfully tapping the tip of my nose with her forefinger.

I was relieved that her enthusiasm for spontaneity matched mine, but I couldn't imagine her mother's matching ours!I pictured Jasmine's mother, a formidable figure with a knack for dramatic flair, swooning dramatically onto the nearest chaise lounge, clutching a handkerchief to her forehead.

DUNES OF THE CAPE

As Jasmine settled on the Harley, her excitement was palpable. Her mother's was not. She stood on the doorstep with a cute pout on her lips, her arms folded loosely across her chest, a furrowed brow, and a slight tilt of her head. She watched us half-heartedly pack the saddlebags onto the Harley, her expression mixed with worry and affection.

Pulling away from the curb, I glanced back, with my hand placed to the left of the centre of my chest, once again expressing my utmost gratitude as she stood there with a faint frown and an intentional expression of her charming disapproval.

As Jasmine's enthusiasm spread to me, I was swept up in the thrill of the ride. Leaning into hairpin turns and sweeping curves, Jasmine exuded an irresistible allure clad in a leather biker jacket and form-fitting denim jeans. The sleek lines of the leather accentuated her curves, hugging her figure in all the right places, adding a rebellious charm to her demeanour. Her sensuality left onlookers mesmerised by her effortless elegance. Despite our age difference, the memory of our kiss lingered with me as we neared our destination. The rugged beauty of Cabo de Gata's dunes, rocky cliffs and sandy beaches came into view along the expanse of the Mediterranean cape; at that moment, I glimpsed her reflection in my rear-view side mirror. Her eyes, sparkling with excitement and anticipation, held me transfixed.

<u>Dear Reader</u>, deciding whether to book one room or two is a significant dilemma; it's uncharted territory where intimacy and comfort are still being established. It's like "testing the waters." Booking one room suggests a desire for closeness and intimacy, while booking separate rooms, though not my preferred option, acknowledges that the dynamic of this relationship is still uncertain.

Taking another spin on this relationship roulette, I asked the receptionist for a double room upon check-in. But before I could finish my sentence, Jasmine interjected with a mischievous shake of her head. "Ah, uh, uh, that's not happening. I have a reservation for two rooms, please," she declared to the bemused receptionist.

Trying to salvage some semblance of dignity, awkwardly clearing my throat, I hastily backtracked. "Right, of course; I was just about to mention that it was two rooms," I mumbled.

Jasmine gave me a sympathetic smile as the receptionist shot me a knowing, smirky glance. As we made our way to separate rooms, who could've known that the simple act of booking a hotel room was akin to navigating through a fine china shop with all the grace of a fucking bull.

The Cabogata Beach Hotel is a luxurious five-star resort on the Cabo de Gata coastline, with stunning views of the Mediterranean Sea. But while the view was spectacular, the true highlight was the exquisite dining experience: dinner served on the beach, with tables adorned in crisp white tablecloths. The coastline and dining areas were illuminated by the soft glow of gas-lit lanterns mounted on bamboo poles, and the lapping of waves against the shore provided a comforting backdrop as we talked for hours.

After dinner, walking barefoot hand in hand along the dunes of the Cape of Cabo de Gata, the feeling of the shifting sand cradling our feet creating a sense of serenity and the faint scent of salt and sea was a feeling I realised I had forgotten. As we wandered deeper into the dunes, my world of looming court dates, incompetent judges and parasitic lawyers seemed to fade away, lulling me into a state of tranquil contentment. I shared my inner secrets with Jasmine, and she spoke to me of her dreams.

With the dunes as our private sanctuary, we stood facing each other. Letting go of Jasmine's trembling hand, I reached out and caressed her cheek, relishing the warmth of her face beneath my touch before our lips met in a searing kiss that deepened as our bodies pressed closer together, merging into a passionate embrace.

That night, we lay in the sand. As Jasmine nestled against me, drifting in and out of sleep, I heard the faint strains of the Pina Colada Song from the beach bar at the hotel (*though not quite the Rupert Holmes version. Better!*) I had always yearned to live the Pina Colada Song when I was with Julia— the juxtaposition of longing for Julia's love and finding unexpected solace in the arms of another had me desperately wishing for a new chapter, story, or book—a chance to start over.

Indeed, they say to be careful what you wish for, and as I lay there with Jasmine, I couldn't help but ponder the truth of those words. The irony wasn't lost on me— longing for something only to find it in the most unexpected places and ways.

The serendipitous turn of events had brought Jasmine into my life.

If you like pina coladas
Makin love in the rain
Skinny-dipping in the ocean
Pampered and entertained
If you like making love at midnight
This can be so insane
And I'm the man you should look for
Come with me and escape

CHAPTER 19
FINAL CHAPTER

During the COVID-19 pandemic, Australia implemented strict entry policies to control the spread of the virus and restock toilet paper on supermarket shelves, all in the name of public health. Initially, Australia slammed its borders shut with flights scarcer than a dingo in downtown Sydney, leaving many of its own citizens stranded abroad and imposed mandatory quarantine measures with returning citizens being ushered into isolation facilities resembling something out of a dystopian sci-fi movie. I wasn't flying back only to be locked away for 14 days of solitary confinement, with nothing but a hotel room and a thank-you bill at the end, as it was for all returning citizens and residents.

To be completely honest, the thought of returning didn't fit well with me anyway.

Since that successful appeal I discussed earlier, Justice Shiva presided over eight more court appearances and concluded with another three days of trial. However, the dynamics of court appearances in the family court underwent significant changes. Gone were the days of bustling courtrooms filled with lawyers, litigants and witnesses as the legal landscape shifted to virtual proceedings conducted via video conferencing platforms such as Zoom. The digital interface of laptops and screens replaced the ritual of entering the courtroom and facing the judge in person.

During one of these remote court appearances, Justice Shiva's virtual courtroom took an unexpected turn. She used a white canvas pull-down screen adorned with the family court emblem, which served as her backdrop. For some reason, with a creak and a groan, the canvas screen suddenly retracted back into the rolling mechanism, lurching backward and exposing a scene that no courtroom etiquette manual could have prepared for. Behind the dignified façade of Justice Shiva's virtual bench lay her bedroom, complete with an unmade bed and scattered belongings strewn about with careless abandon.

You have got to give her credit: Justice Shiva, ever the epitome of composure, attempted to salvage the situation with a sheepish smile. She muted her microphone and hastily left the virtual courtroom so she could make a hurried attempt to wrestle the rebellious backdrop back into submission. It seemed like a fitting bit of slapstick, the dreaded courtrooms that had loomed over my days for so many years, giving way to a collapsing set in a bedroom. And in just a few Zoom sessions, Justice Shiva used an actual understanding of the law and common sense to overturn Smallcock's mistakes and finally bring the whole, grinding, massive process to a halt, acknowledging the obvious (that I wasn't a threat to the children and that Julia shouldn't get the company) and enacting the division of the marital assets (which had largely been spent during the divorce.) The fireworks that had raged over our divorce for years ended with a fizzle.

What a journey it's been.

AFTERWORD

With each stroke of the pen while writing this book (that's right, I did it the old-fashioned way), I've invited you to embark on a profoundly personal journey, offering an unfiltered glimpse into my pain, anguish, and frustration with a system that often feels irreparably flawed. Through candid reflection and unflinching honesty, I cried, unleashing a torrent of emotions that had laid dormant, buried beneath layers of time and experience. Within these pages, I lay bare the raw emotions and tangled complexities that often accompany the dissolution of a marriage. I did this because I wanted to remind you that you are not alone. Meeting each of you personally isn't feasible, of course; that's precisely why I decided to write and share Divorced Virgin- not just for you, but with you.

If only I could warmly embrace you and assure you that brighter days are ahead. My words are here to provide you with solace and encouragement. Jasmine, who is now my dear wife, gifted me my Limited Writer's Edition Mont Blanc pen as a gesture from our son and encouraged me to write, and I am forever grateful to her and my son.

The book focussed on my experience, of course, and the unique challenges that men face during divorce. But here's a gentle plea for all the ex-wives and women going through the process: please resist the allure of vengeance. In seeking retribution on a partner with whom you once shared a history of love and companionship, you only sow the seeds of further regret, discord, and pain. It will make the process so much worse for both of you. I promise you.

Throughout Divorced Virgin, I often described divorce as the death of a marriage, though I've said very little about the funeral procession of regrets that follows in its wake. Regret is a cruel master, a constant reminder of misguided decisions that led us to this point. It is a weight of missed opportunities and unspoken apologies, carried as a constant companion of what could have been. The aftermath of divorce is a lonely place with shattered dreams and fractured hearts. One of the most poignant regrets you will carry is the toll the legal battle took on your children and the perception of your pursuit of justice that your solicitors will undoubtedly instil upon you that will cause your spiral into a financial quagmire.

My ex-wife, Julia, was unwavering in her refusal to accept any terms or settlements I proposed, no matter how reasonable. This obstinacy is why we had to drag ourselves through more than fifty court appearances in the family court. Despite my earnest efforts to negotiate and reach a compromise, Julia remained resolute in pursuing what she deemed rightfully hers. Ultimately, Justice Shiva's ruling brought a harsh reality to light. Ultimately, Julia was awarded less than half of what I had initially offered at the outset of our divorce proceedings. All that sound and fury signifying nothing.

To those facing similar challenges, I urge you to consider the longer-term consequences of your actions. While the temptation to fight for what you believe is rightfully yours may be strong, the toll it takes on your family, both emotionally and financially, is a heavy burden. In the end, neither of you wins.

To those who find themselves on the precipice of divorce, I urge you to heed this cautionary tale. If you can negotiate a settlement without going to court and fighting it out, do it. While the allure of litigation may promise vindication and recompense, the reality is often far from it. No one emerges victorious except for the lawyers who profit from our conflicts. This bitter truth became increasingly evident to me as my journey in Divorced Virgin unfolded over the years.

I did not make the decision to represent myself in court lightly, but as the costs of legal representation soared, it became increasingly clear that I had no choice but to stand alone in the courtroom. Julia's legal team unnecessarily imposed a myriad of fees upon our collective asset pool, including repeated expert valuations, financial audits, and family reports. In addition to these expenses, there were the costs associated with expert testimonies aimed at refuting falsified documents, scrutinising accounting reports, and preparing and submitting appeals. Julia's self-inflicted mountain of legal fees left her with _nothing_ except a half share of the beachside property in Spain, which still requires resolution in Spanish Courts.

Julia's experience is a cautionary tale and underscores the importance of reading Divorced Virgin with vigilance before engaging in any legal representation.

Unless there is a legitimate and significant risk to your safety or your children, I implore you to prioritise open and honest communication with your soon-to-be ex-husband. While it may be tempting to make false claims or seek an intervention order (IVO) out of anger or frustration, it is essential to consider the long-term repercussions. Engaging in such actions will require the court to order family reports (for the safety and well-being of the children) at a significant cost to you when you know he has been a great father. Further, once you make those accusations, all communication with your soon-to-be ex must be done in writing through both your lawyers, incurring hefty hourly fees for even the most mundane and tedious exchanges.

As we close the final pages, reflecting on our tumultuous journey, I extend my heartfelt gratitude. Your presence, your resilience and determination to not get screwed, and your willingness to engage have given purpose to this narrative. My sincerest hope is that in sharing my story, I have offered solace, inspiration, and perhaps a glimmer of guidance for those walking a similar path. I've sought to impart a message of resilience, hope, and the importance of introspection.

I extend my heartfelt gratitude to each <u>Dear Reader</u> who has followed along. Your empathy for my deeply personal truths, initial hesitations, and later frustrations and vulnerabilities has inspired me to go beyond simply recounting events.

Let me leave you with these words: know you are not alone. Your journey as a Divorced Virgin holds value. Carry forward the lessons learned, wisdom gained, and unwavering belief in your resilience.

DIVORCED VIRGIN

www.ingramcontent.com/pod-product-compliance
Lightning Source LLC
Chambersburg PA
CBHW072157070526
44585CB00015B/1191